GREAT PASSENGER SHIPS
1920–1930

WILLIAM H. MILLER

The
History
Press

For Marie Radigan

Dear friend, superb teacher and the most
wonderful mother

New York's Chelsea Piers in 1929, with *Île de France, De Grasse,
Pennland, Olympic, Cedric* and *Duchess of Bedford* at berth (Author's
Collection).

First published 2014

The History Press
The Mill, Brimscombe Port
Stroud, Gloucestershire, GL5 2QG
www.thehistorypress.co.uk

© William H. Miller, 2014

The right of William H. Miller to be identified as the Author
of this work has been asserted in accordance with the
Copyright, Designs and Patents Act 1988.

British Library Cataloguing in Publication Data.
A catalogue record for this book is available from the British Library.

ISBN 978 0 7524 8809 7

Typesetting and origination by The History Press
Printed in India

Cover Illustrations.
Front: Statendam (Stephen Card).
Back: Vulcania (Stephen Card).

CONTENTS

FOREWORD

The 1920s were a period of revival, rejuvenation – certainly rebuilding – and notation. The United States, for example, entered the 'big leagues' of transatlantic travel with the introduction of the 59,000-ton *Leviathan* in 1923 – now America had a superliner of its own. Furthermore, the American Merchant Lines marked the introduction of the combination passenger-cargo ships – 'combo ships' as they were called – with a balanced blend of passengers and freight.

Across the Atlantic, the likes of Cunard turned to more moderate new tonnage, with their large class of single-stackers, such as the 20,000-ton *Scythia*, but then the French moved forward with the luxurious *Paris* and later, in 1927, with the decoratively innovative *Île de France*; with her Art Deco styling she was the great divide in passenger ship style and decor. In 1929, however, the Dutch jumped ahead with the otherwise traditional *Statendam*, while the Italians created their biggest liners yet – the 32,000-ton near-sisters *Augustus* and *Roma*. The Swedes commissioned the diesel-driven *Gripsholm* in 1925, when motor liners would become the new vogue, but it was the Germans, rather quickly recovering from the devastation of the First World War, who produced two very important superliners: the 50,000-ton near-sisters *Bremen* and *Europa*. Mighty ships in every sense, they were also the fastest ships afloat for a time.

Elsewhere, to South America, and Africa and to Australia and Eastern ports, bigger, finer and faster liners were created, such as the mighty *Alcantara* and *Asturias*, which were added to the run down to Rio and Buenos Aires, while P&O commissioned the striking *Viceroy of India* for colonial service to Bombay. Japan went forward with the likes of the *Asama Maru* and service to Hawaii was greatly enhanced with the introduction of the noted *Malolo*.

The '20s was indeed a very interesting and significant time for ocean liners. Bill Miller has produced another fine and insightful book on our favorite topic: passenger ships. It is a great pleasure to read over the pages.

Bon voyage!

Captain James McNamara
President, National Cargo Bureau
New York, 2014

INTRODUCTION

When the First World War officially ended on that November morning in 1918, records of devastation and destruction were perhaps even more dramatic. In the shipping industry, the mighty Cunard Line, one of the biggest operators on the famed Atlantic run to North America, had lost no less than thirty ships. Equal in size, the huge Hamburg America Line and North German Lloyd fleets were in ruins. Holland's intended new flagship had gone to the bottom and two of Britain's mightiest liners, the *Lusitania* and the *Britannic*, had also been sunk. The destruction was quite staggering.

No other war had changed the map of Europe so dramatically. Alone, four empires disappeared – the German, Austro-Hungarian, Ottoman and Russian. Four dynasties went as well. Belgium and Serbia were badly damaged and the French had nearly 1½ million dead. Of all European soldiers involved, 7 million were permanently disabled. Germany lost 15 per cent of its male population.

There were positive developments, of course. America grew significantly as a military force. There were changes in technology, medicine and working-class standards. While Britain lost 40 per cent of her merchant fleet, there was a considerable reparation fleet of seized German tonnage. The biggest liner in the world, the 56,000grt *Bismarck*, was taken by the British and subsequently completed as the *Majestic* of the London-based White Star Line. Interestingly, of Britain's six largest and finest express liners of the 1920s, three of them were ex-German. Equally, America had its largest passenger liner ever, the former German *Vaterland*, which became the *Leviathan*.

By 1919–20, as the dust of war finally settled, a sense of moderation, even caution, had taken hold over the shipping industry and in almost all corners of the globe. First and foremost, trading conditions had changed – or were changing. The enthusiasm for, say, those big, fast 'floating palaces' of the pre-war years were shunted, if temporarily, aside. The biggest, fastest liners would not come for almost another decade, until 1929, with the 49,000grt, German near-sisters, *Europa* and *Bremen*.

No British shipowner planned superliners in the early twenties, but instead looked to more moderate, medium-sized and sometimes even unpretentious passenger ships. The famed Belfast shipbuilder Harland & Wolff produced a series of 16,000-tonners for general account (one eventually went to the Dominion Line, one to White Star and two to Holland America). Even mighty Cunard produced a series of single-stackers: useful, comfortable, profitable, but largely unnoteworthy.

There were some cases of noted growth. The Swedes, for example, jumped forward with the 18,000grt *Gripsholm* in 1925 and then, bigger still, the 20,000grt *Kungsholm* three years later. From the Mediterranean, Italy began creating a much stronger presence in its services to New York and the east coast of South America. The 24,300grt sisters *Giulio Cesare* and *Duilio* were created in 1923–24. Bigger ships followed –

such as the *Conte Biancamano*, *Conte Grande*, *Saturnia*, *Vulcania*, *Roma* and, the biggest motor liner yet built, the 32,650grt *Augustus* of 1927. There were even plans filled with high enthusiasm for Italy's first and only four-stackers – the 2,700-passenger *Andrea Doria* and *Camillo di Cavour*. Those plans were abandoned soon after the war ended, in 1919.

The French made one of the greatest impressions with the stunning *Paris*, a 34,500-tonner and then the all-important, standard-setting *Île de France*, even larger at 43,100 tons. Her decorative style, based on an exhibition in Paris in 1925, two years before the ship itself was commissioned, created new ocean liner style. In retrospect, the *Île de France* was the beginning of Art Deco on the high seas. Almost all Atlantic liners quickly followed in her decorative wake. After long construction delays, Holland replaced its lost flagship with the new, three-funnel, *Statendam*.

Germany revived steadily, even if with mostly moderate-sized liners such as Hamburg America Line's 'Big Four' – *Albert Ballin*, *Deutschland*, *Hamburg* and *New York*. North German Lloyd had an even splashier revival with the 32,500grt *Columbus* of 1924. She was the prompt for two further, similar-sized ships, but which were redesigned as the far larger *Europa* and *Bremen*. A third German shipowner, the Hamburg South America Line, had a surge from mass European migration to South America with five sister ships of the 13,800grt *Monte Rosa* class and then finished with the grand 27,500grt *Cap Arcona*, one of the most legendary German liners ever.

At the western end of the Atlantic trade, America's presence increased considerably in the twenties, especially with the creation of the United States Lines.

Cruising grew in popularity in the 1920s and especially on long, luxurious itineraries. Cunard offered the first full world cruise from New York in 1922; by the end of the decade, there were ten such sailings. Even big, celebrated Atlantic liners went cruising – such as the *Mauretania*, *Aquitania* and *Homeric* – on long winter voyages to the sun. A market for more club-like, smaller ship cruises grew as well with the building of the 190-passenger *Stella Polaris* and, in Britain, the creation of the 354-bed *Arandora Star*. In the Pacific, the sparkling new *Malolo* greatly improved Hawaiian tourism.

Government-supported colonial services increased and improved in the twenties – such as Britain to India, Holland to the East Indies and France to Indochina. The likes of P&O and others greatly expanded passenger links to Australia and the Far East while the likes of the Union-Castle Line strengthened its services to Africa.

The pace in passenger ship construction continued and reached a high point at the end of the decade with Germany's *Bremen* and *Europa*, superliners of great size, speed and luxury. They were a hint to the future, to the 1930s, to an age of the *Empress of Britain*, *Rex*, *Conte di Savoia*, *Normandie*, *Queen Mary* and many, many more. The great story of the grand liners would continue!

Bill Miller
Secaucus, New Jersey
2014

1

EXPRESS LINERS ON THE ATLANTIC

The First World War was devastating to Europe – enormous numbers of lives had been lost, nations bankrupted, borders redrawn and old standards thrown aside. In shipping, over one-third of the world passenger fleet was gone, victims of war. While the likes of the British fleet had some gaping holes (such as the losses of the superliners *Lusitania* for Cunard and the *Britannic* at White Star), the once huge German liner fleet was devastated, either destroyed in enemy action or carved up as reparations to the Allies. In Holland, the *Statendam*, the nation's largest liner yet, was at the bottom of the sea and the completion of France's *Paris* was delayed by five years. Across the Atlantic, America was left with a large fleet of seized ex-German passenger ships, including the giant German *Vaterland*, which became the *Leviathan*. More changes were ahead.

The major transatlantic companies wanted – sometimes almost urgently – to re-establish services to New York and this included the express run using the biggest, fastest, fanciest liners. The mainstay – useful to loyal first-class travellers, businessmen, politicians and the new age of Hollywood celebrities – were the fast, six-day passages between Southampton, Cherbourg and New York. Both

Cunard and White Star were deeply interested but needed three sizeable liners to maintain this run – and with great reliability as well. Cunard reopened this service in 1920 with the immensely popular *Mauretania*, still the fastest liner afloat and therefore adding greatly to her following; then there was the *Aquitania*, dubbed 'the Ship Beautiful' for her good looks both

Cunard's giant *Berengaria*, one of the most popular big Atlantic liners of all time, arriving at New York's Pier 54, at the foot of West 14th Street. The date is 1925 and the *Minnetonka* is on the far left, at Pier 58, and then the French *De Grasse* is at Pier 57 (Author's Collection).

inside and out; and the newly acquired *Berengaria*, the former *Imperator* of the Hamburg America Line and allocated as part of reparations. Each of these ships was highly successful and profitable in its own right.

The 31,938grt *Mauretania* also had beautiful interiors, representing the very best in design and style from both Britain and Europe. The woods that were used, for example, were selected from British and French forests. The carvings were done to exacting details. Decorative themes ranged from French Renaissance to English country. The liner's first-class main lounge was one of her finest spaces, being capped by a large domed skylight and featuring a marble fireplace at the far end. The first-class dining room was a two-deck-high affair, with tables on each level. It was likened to those found in the finest hotels in London, Paris and New York. Designed as a retreat on summer afternoons or as a retreat on grey winter voyages, the veranda cafe was a creation of greenery, wicker furniture and glossy linoleum floors.

In all, the *Mauretania* carried 2,335 passengers as built – 560 in first class, 475 second class and 1,300 third class. Post-war changes had included the great decline in migrant passengers due to American quotas beginning in 1924. Afterward, third class – with some dressing up with paint, curtains and more comfortable furnishings – had to appeal to discount tourists, in particular the new and growing numbers of Americans heading for Europe. It was, in a way, the new bargain way to travel abroad.

A panoramic view of Lower Manhattan and the Hudson River, dated 1925. New York was the ocean liner capital of the world and the 919ft-long *Berengaria* is outbound in mid-Hudson. The 790ft-tall Woolworth Building, then the world's tallest skyscraper, is to the right (Author's Collection).

The beloved *Mauretania* outbound from New York in a view dated June 1931 (Richard Faber Collection).

End of the line! Ready to begin her final voyage to the scrappers, the veteran *Mauretania* is seen at Southampton on 7 May 1935 (Cronican-Arroyo Collection).

Picturesque setting! The beautiful *Aquitania* is seen in this poetic photo at Villefranche. She was then the largest liner to cruise the Mediterranean (Cronican-Arroyo Collection).

The four-funnel, 901ft-long *Aquitania* was a beloved ship for all of her days. Commissioned in 1914 just before the war started, she was quickly taken up for military duties – serving as a troopship as well as a hospital ship. Her heroic record made her even more popular in the years after the war ended. Her first-class quarters, sumptuously restored, were as glorious as ever. Surely, the columned Palladian lounge, two decks in height, was one of the most beautiful rooms ever to put to sea. Another was the Jacobean smoking room, which was copied from the Royal Naval College at Greenwich.

'Only the smartest dogs prefer to cross the Atlantic on board the *Berengaria*' was one slogan of the day. Despite her German heritage, she had a chicness about her, a 'certain something', according to one frequent traveller, that made her immensely popular. One tycoon booked a suite aboard her for five years. He wanted it just for his own use. At 52,226 tons and 919ft in length, she was the largest Cunarder until the advent of the *Queen Mary* in 1936. Even with her barely disguised, rather heavy Teutonic interiors, she was thought to be one of Britain's very finest liners. The Prince of Wales (later Edward VIII and then the Duke of Windsor), Queen Marie of Rumania, Mayor Jimmy Walker of New York City and Marlene Dietrich were among her more famous passengers.

Laid up at Hamburg throughout the First World War, she was actually taken by the Americans as reparations in 1919 and briefly sailed as the troop transport USS *Imperator* before being allocated to the British. She actually sailed under her German name for Cunard (1919–20) until fully refitted and renamed *Berengaria* in 1921. Cunard was rightfully proud of her and described her as:

Almost a fifth of a mile long she is. And she accommodates over 2,000 appreciative persons. She is a grand, big, ship-shape ship. From the superb breath and length of her colossal decks, the ferryboats of the commuters are minimised to pigmy-proportions and the terrier-like activities of the little barking tugboats take on a toy-like character. All smug land comparisons to the *Berengaria* are odious.

In direct competition with Cunard, the White Star Line had three express liners of its own. The 56,551grt *Majestic* was the flagship, but far more importantly ranked as the largest liner afloat. This brought her added passengers. Passengers all loved great distinctions among the ships they sailed and especially liked sending postcards and greetings from 'the world's biggest ship of any kind'. Carrying up to 2,145 passengers in three classes, the *Majestic* was intended to be the third of Germany's pre-war giants – the *Bismarck*. She was not completed, however, spent the war years in Hamburg and was acquired by the Allies once the conflict ended. She was later allocated to White Star as compensation for the loss of their 48,100grt *Britannic* in 1916. As the renamed *Majestic*, the 956ft-long liner was honoured, in 1922, by a royal visit from King George V and Queen Mary.

First-class quarters aboard the *Majestic* were expectedly luxurious. Her main lounge was a room of great beauty with oak-panelled walls and hand-carved ornamentation, and offset by tall French windows. The columned indoor pool, done in Pompeiian style, had a full depth of 10ft. The dome-ceilinged dining room ranked as one of the largest of its kind at sea and could seat some 700 at a time. Overall, her passenger

The world's largest liner, White Star's 56,600grt *Majestic*, is outbound at New York in a view dated 1924 (Albert Wilhelmi Collection).

accommodations were equivalent, according to White Star promotional literature, to 400 eight-room houses.

The 46,439grt *Olympic* had an Edwardian beauty of carved woods, crystal lamps and highly polished lino flooring. Built in 1911, the 882ft-long ship was, of course, a sister ship to the ill-fated *Titanic*.

The smallest of White Star's prominent trio, the 34,352grt *Homeric* might have been North German Lloyd's *Columbus*, but was never completed and instead her hull was acquired by the Allies. Allocated to the British and then to White Star, the 2,766-passenger ship entered British flag service in the winter of 1922.

There was a seventh superliner: America's otherwise largely unsuccessful *Leviathan*, operated by the New York-based United States Lines. She had been commissioned in 1914 as *Hamburg* America's *Vaterland*, but then seized at her berth in New York when the US entered the war in April 1917. She operated under Yankee colours with several disadvantages: she did not

Below: A stern view of the *Laurentic*, built for White Star in 1927 and the last coal-burner on the Atlantic run. This scene in mid-Hudson River is dated 31 January 1931 (Richard Faber Collection).

Above: Farewell from New York's Pier 61: White Star's beautiful *Olympic* departs on a winter crossing to Cherbourg and Southampton (Cronican-Arroyo Collection).

Right: Afternoon arrival! White Star's *Homeric* arrives at New York's Chelsea Piers in a photo dated December 1931 (Richard Faber Collection).

Left: Air travel is a distant hint of the future in this 1920s' view of Southampton. Three superliners are in port: the *Leviathan* and *Olympic* are together in the Ocean Dock while the *Mauretania* is resting in the port's floating dry dock (Author's Collection).

Right: America's largest and most luxurious liner to date, the 59,000grt *Leviathan*, prepares to depart from Pier 86, New York, on her maiden Atlantic crossing. The date is 4 July 1923 (Author's Collection).

have a running mate, American service was said to be inferior to those on European liners and the higher cost of operating US flag vessels.

Fares in the 1920s aboard these express liners were listed as $185 in first class, $90 in cabin class and $50 in third class.

The era of this generation of the 'floating palaces', as they were so aptly dubbed, ended with the onset of the Depression and the 1930s. In the wake of the Wall Street Crash in October 1929, transatlantic passenger loads began to fall steadily – from 1 million travellers in 1930 to 500,000 by 1935. Even the biggest, grandest and once most popular liners were struggling. There were empty cabins on just about every crossing. The *Mauretania* was soon detoured to running inexpensive, overnight 'booze cruises' from New York. Americans could sail out past the 3-mile limit and drink legally (avoiding Prohibition rules), and then somehow walk off the ship the next morning after breakfast. It all seemed quite affordable at $10 per person. The *Berengaria* made low-cost trips as well – long weekends up to Halifax or down to Bermuda. She was soon dubbed the 'Bargain-area'. In Britain,

the *Olympic* made one-night cruises as well, priced from £1 per passenger. The *Aquitania* spent her winters on long jaunts around the Mediterranean, ferrying a few of the world's last remaining millionaires, while the *Homeric* was now making more cruises than crossings. Indeed, the grand days had passed – if temporarily.

Except for the *Aquitania*, which survived through the Second World War and returned to service until 1950, this group of liners was all but gone by the late 1930s. The *Mauretania* went to the breakers in 1934, the *Olympic* and *Homeric* in 1935, while the *Majestic* was decommissioned in 1936 and later became a naval training school. Finally, the *Berengaria* went for scrap in 1938. It has often been suggested and written that these ships, if they had been kept in reserve, would have been most useful as troopships, beginning in September 1939, at the start of the Second World War.

Transatlantic crossings were frequent and varied in the twenties. A sample sailing schedule from New York for Thursday to Saturday, 6–8 September 1928 read:

Contemporary amenity: a new nightclub was installed aboard the refitted *Leviathan* in 1923 (Cronican-Arroyo Collection).

The sitting room veranda in one of the finest suites aboard the 950ft-long *Leviathan*. The fare for this sumptuous accommodation was $1,500 per person in the mid-1920s (Cronican-Arroyo Collection).

Thu Sep 6	9:00am	*Karlsruhe*	to Bremen
Thu Sep 6	11:00am	*La Bourdonnais*	to Bordeaux
Thu Sep 6	5:00pm	*Thuringia*	to Bremen
Thu Sep 6	11:59pm	*Tuscania*	to London
Fri Sep 7	11:00am	*Suffren*	to Le Havre
Fri Sep 7	5:00pm	*Luetzow*	to Bremen
Fri Sep 7	11:59pm	*Île de France*	to Le Havre
Fri Sep 7	11:59pm	*Homeric*	to So'hampton
Fri Sep 7	11:59pm	*Pennland*	to Antwerp
Sat Sep 8	11:00am	*Minnewaska*	to London
Sat Sep 8	11:00am	*Oscar II*	to Copenhagen
Sat Sep 8	11:00am	*Rotterdam*	to Rotterdam
Sat Sep 8	11:30am	*Celtic*	to Liverpool
Sat Sep 8	11:30am	*Carinthia*	to Liverpool
Sat Sep 8	Noon	*Transylvania*	to Glasgow
Sat Sep 8	Noon	*Conte Grande*	to Genoa
Sat Sep 8	Noon	*Gripsholm*	to Gothenburg
Sat Sep 8	Noon	*Columbus*	to Brem'hvn
Sat Sep 8	3:00pm	*Polonia*	to Danzig
Sat Sep 8	5:00pm	*Albert Ballin*	to Hamburg

New medium-sized passenger ships continued to come on line as well. White Star Line, which seemed never quite to recover from the tragic loss of the *Titanic* back in April 1912, built only two new passenger ships in the twenties. The 16,500grt *Doric* was added in 1922 and then, slightly larger, the 18,700grt *Laurentic* came into service in 1927. The *Doric* was one of the sadder victims of the Depression of the next decade. After a serious collision resulting in extensive damages in September 1935, the 13-year-old liner was sold, without any reluctance, for scrap rather than repaired. The *Laurentic* was a dated vessel when new – she was the last coal-burning liner under the British Ensign.

The economics of running passenger ships became severe, almost ruthless, in the 1930s. Atlantic Transport Line built twin sister ships, the *Minnetonka* and *Minnewaska* – large combination passenger-cargo ships for London–New York service and carrying 369 all-first-class passengers – that were all but complete failures. These 22,000grt sisters were sold to scrappers in 1933–34 when they were just a decade old.

The Swedish American Line was innovative, however, and produced two very successful, long-lived liners. When the 17,993grt *Gripsholm* was built in 1925, the company decided on something unique, rather novel – instead

The slightly larger *Kungsholm* followed in 1928 and she too became a very popular ship. Apart from crossings, her cruises were renowned – from a week to Bermuda, two and three weeks in the Caribbean, forty-five days to the North Cape to seventy-five days around Africa. She was sold, however, to the US Government just after the Japanese attack on Pearl Harbor, in January 1942. She then became the troopship USS *John Ericsson*, managed by the United States Lines for the then War Shipping Administration. Valiantly, she sailed worldwide. After the war, in March 1947, she was badly damaged by fire while berthed at New York, at Pier 90, and just across the shed from the mighty *Queen Elizabeth*. Having no further use for the 21,554grt ship, she was resold to her Swedish owners, who in turn promptly resold her to the Home Lines, then an infant multinational company in which the Swedes had a financial interest. The 609ft-long ship went to Genoa and was refitted as the *Italia*. She became one of Home Lines' most successful and popular ships. She finished her days as a moored hotel ship in the Bahamas before being sold to Spanish ship-breakers in 1965.

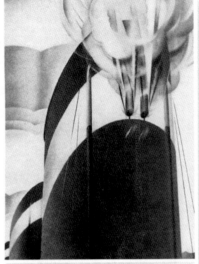

An advertisement for crossings on the United States Lines, dated October 1929 (*National Geographic* magazine).

Crossing and cruises German-American style: an advertisement for the joint services of the United American Lines and the Hamburg American Line – the date, March 1925 (*National Geographic* magazine).

of traditional steam turbines, the 573ft-long liner would be propelled by diesels. When commissioned, the 1,557-passenger *Gripsholm* became the first motor liner on the North Atlantic. Soon, other liners would follow with diesel propulsion. The *Gripsholm*, a very popular Atlantic as well as cruising liner, survived the Second World War and, later, in 1955, became West Germany's first post-war liner, the *Berlin* of North German Lloyd. She sailed until scrapped in Italy in 1966.

This Summer it's the "European Week-End"

Europe has taken its place in the category of the casual week-end affair. Seventeen days over and back—with four days for sightseeing and shopping in London and Paris —think of that! Many are adding three days to their summer vacations and treating themselves to a glimpse of Europe, with two ocean voyages for brimming measure. Sail from New York on a week-end— spend that week-end on the ocean and the next in Europe. Book on the *Majestic*, the world's largest ship, or the popular *Olympic*. For a more leisurely crossing, there's the *Homeric*, the *Belgenland*, the *Minnewaska*, *Minnetonka*, and a wide choice of moderately priced Cabin liners. The service is impeccable—the cost can be fitted to your purse.

For full information apply to No. 1 Broadway, New York City; 180 No. Michigan Ave., Chicago; 460 Market St., San Francisco; our offices elsewhere or any authorized steamship agent.

WHITE STAR LINE
RED STAR LINE · ATLANTIC TRANSPORT LINE
INTERNATIONAL MERCANTILE MARINE COMPANY

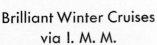

Brilliant Winter Cruises via I. M. M.

Sixth World Cruise of the *Belgenland*, largest, finest liner that has ever circled the globe—from New York Dec. 20, over a route proved perfect on her five former cruises. 133 days—28,000 miles. Operated jointly by Red Star Line and American Express Co. $1750 (up).

Also four 46-day cruises to the Mediterranean by White Star Line during January, February and March. The itinerary includes the high spots of tourist interest bordering this glamorous inland sea. $695 (up.)

Likewise a series of novel 11-day cruises to Havana, Nassau and Bermuda by Red Star liner *Lapland*. Sailing Dec. 28; Jan. 11 and 25; Feb. 8 and 22; Mar. 8. $175 (up).

White Star compared a crossing of the Atlantic to a casual weekend affair (*National Geographic* magazine).

Invigorating days at sea: deck games aboard Canadian Pacific's *Duchess of York* in a scene dated 1929 (Canadian Pacific Steamships).

Aft deck spaces on board the giant *Berengaria* (Cunard Line).

Celebrity passengers were aboard almost every crossing of the big express liners. In this view, dated 19 May 1922, Sinclair Lewis and his family arrive in New York aboard the *Aquitania* (Author's Collection).

Resembling a much larger line: with her three funnels (the first and third were actually dummies), the 17,000grt *Caledonia* was used in Anchor Line's Glasgow–New York service (Michael Cassar).

Atlantic Transport Line's *Minnetonka*, a 21,998grt ship built in 1924 but then scrapped prematurely only ten years later, in 1934, due to the Depression (Gillespie-Faber Collection).

A second life! Sweden's *Gripsholm* of 1925 became West Germany's first passenger liner when she was commissioned as the *Berlin* in 1955. Operated by a reviving North German Lloyd, the ship (which was lengthened to 590ft in 1949) is seen here at Bremerhaven in a photo dated January 1955 (Cronican-Arroyo Collection).

Sweden's 20,223grt *Kungsholm* of 1928 became the *Italia* of the multinational Home Lines in 1947 (Author's Collection).

Small combination passenger-cargo ships such as the 7,430grt *American Merchant* also served on the Atlantic run. Carrying seventy-four one-class passengers in service between New York and London, the 1920-built ship is seen here departing from the 2nd Street Pier in Hoboken in a view dated 1931 (Richard Faber Collection).

Scotland's River Clyde was the birthplace of many great passenger ships until the 1960s. This poetic view on a misty afternoon looks across to the last remains of the John Brown shipyard at Clydebank. The date is July 2003 (Author's Collection).

2

REBUILDING: CUNARD'S SINGLE-STACKERS

The First World War had been especially hard on the Cunard Line. Altogether, the company lost eleven passenger ships – including the superliner *Lusitania*. Reinforcing and rebuilding its post-war fleet including its auxiliary services to Boston, Halifax and on the seasonal trade to the St Lawrence, to Quebec City and Montreal, the Liverpool-based firm also felt that more moderate ships – more practical, useful and therefore economic – were ideally suited to the changed trading conditions on the North Atlantic. The age of mass migration to the United States, particularly to New York, was about to end (with new, stricter American immigration quotas imposed in 1924) and be replaced by a demand for low-fare, tourist-class quarters. A new age of tourism to Europe was an outcome of the First World War. There were also first-class passengers who wanted comfort, even luxury, but not especially on board the big express liners. And so, Cunard embarked on a very ambitious post-war rebuilding programme – fourteen new passenger ships in all.

There was one 'misfit' in the group, however: the *Albania* of 1920. She was the least successful and soon sold off. She was followed by a group of five, very successful ships: three identical sisters – *Scythia*, *Samaria* and *Laconia* of 1921–22; and two modified sisters, the *Franconia* and *Carinthia*, of 1923

and 1925. A modified version was the *Tyrrhenia*, actually ordered by the rival Anchor Line and completed in 1922. Her name was soon changed to the more popular *Lancastria*. The design of the 20,000-ton *Scythia* class was reworked, changed and readapted as six sisters of the 14,000 ton 'A-Class' – *Antonia*, *Ausonia*, *Andania*, *Aurania*, *Ascania* and *Alaunia*, built between 1922 and 1925. Altogether, these fourteen ships were Cunard's 'intermediates' – their single-stackers of the twenties.

The 19,730grt *Scythia* was the forerunner of this intermediate fleet and all were distinguished by each having a single, very slender funnel. Laid down in 1919, just after the war ended, her construction at the Vickers yard at Barrow-in-Furness was so beset with labour problems and strikes that she had to be completed at Rotterdam. Once in service, she reopened Cunard's run between Liverpool, Queenstown (later renamed Cobh), Boston and New York. Designed for three classes, her passenger accommodation was configured as 337 cabin class, 331 tourist class and 1,538 third class. The 624ft-long *Scythia* was a popular ship from the start and soon praised for her accommodation, especially in cabin class. The garden lounge was fitted with lush greenery, the oval lounge was capped by a domed skylight and

A 1933 view: A classic single-stacker, Cunard's 1,650-passenger *Carinthia* departs from New York, but on a cruise for which capacity was specially reduced to 450 all first class. Lower Manhattan's Woolworth Building and, to the right, the Singer Building stand out (Richard Faber Collection).

the gymnasium was said to be among the very best on the Atlantic. There were added novelties such as the American bar (a very popular amenity with Prohibition-struck American passengers) and private bathrooms in almost all cabin-class staterooms – then a rare feature in even the largest, grandest liners.

The 16-knot *Scythia* had a long life with Cunard. After serving during the Second World War as a trooper, she returned to the Canadian service until 1957. She went to breakers in Scotland early in 1958 after having been with Cunard for thirty-seven years.

Ships such as the *Scythia*, *Samaria* and *Laconia* were also popular because of their more leisurely eight- to ten-day crossings. Their decor continued to lure travellers, however. On board the 2,180-passenger *Laconia*, the cabin-class accommodation included a writing room done in Adam style, a main lounge in Queen Anne and a smoking room designed to resemble an old English inn, complete with red brick fireplace. All three ships were purposely designed to spend much of the year on the class-divided Atlantic run, but the winters on all-one-class cruises. Especially in the hard-pressed

Bon voyage! The 623ft-long *Franconia*, dressed in flags, departs from New York's Pier 54 bound for a sixty-five-day cruise around the Mediterranean. Long, luxurious cruises were becoming increasingly popular in the twenties (Author's Collection).

1930s, when Atlantic travel dropped off considerably, these ships were sent often on fourteen- to twenty-one-day cruises – to the Caribbean, the Atlantic Isles and West Africa, the Mediterranean and to the Norwegian fjords and northern cities. Occasionally, they did longer cruises, months in duration, such as the *Laconia*'s fifty-two-night cruise to South America from Liverpool, beginning in January 1938. Overall on that voyage, she logged 14,000 miles.

While both the *Scythia* and *Samaria* survived the Second World War, the 19,860grt *Laconia* was a casualty. She was converted to an armed merchant cruiser in September 1939, soon after the hostilities began, and later to a high-capacity troopship. She was torpedoed off West Africa in September 1942. At the time, she was carrying 1,800 Italian prisoners of war and 900 others. Only 100 survived, being rescued by nearby Nazi submarines. The prisoners were given unexpected freedom; the British crewmembers were sent to internment in Morocco.

Slightly larger at 20,100grt, the *Franconia*, commissioned in the summer of 1923, and the *Carinthia*, delivered two years later, were improved versions of the previous three. There were differences in design as well as improvements in the passenger accommodation. With an added eye on long, luxurious cruising, facilities aboard the 623ft-long *Franconia* included a two-deck-high smoking room that was styled after the fifteenth-century residence of El Greco; another lounge done in early English style; twin garden lounges; and such special amenities as a chocolate shop, health centre and even a racquetball court. In warm waters, a portable swimming pool was erected on deck and filled with sea water.

From the start, both the *Franconia* and *Carinthia* – both later repainted with more tropical, all-white hulls – were used for $10-a-day cruises to Bermuda, Nassau, the Caribbean and South America. They later became very popular for their longer, more diverse voyages as well – such as eight weeks around continental South America, ten weeks around Africa, forty-five days to the Scandinavia and the North Cape and as long as 165 days around the world. On those circumnavigations, the ships often departed in December and returned in May or June and en route might spend as long as seven days in Japan and ten nights in India. Often, they sailed east-about – from New York across to the Mediterranean, then through the Suez Canal and along the Middle East and Indian Ocean, Southeast Asia, the Far East, across the Pacific via Hawaii to California and then down to Mexico and home to New York via the Panama Canal. Fares in 1930 began at $2,000 for a five and a half-month-long cruise.

The *Franconia*, outfitted as a 3,000-capacity troopship in September 1939, had her heroics. On a voyage to the Mediterranean that October, she collided with another large troopship, Royal Mail Lines' *Alcantara*. The Cunarder was later repaired, but more danger lay ahead. The following June, she was hit in an air attack while in evacuation service off western France. Later, near the war's end in the winter of 1945, the 16½-knot *Franconia* had special duties: she was sent to the Mediterranean and then to Yalta in the Black Sea to await top-secret instructions. She was to serve as the floating headquarters for Winston Churchill and his staff during the historic Yalta Conference. A series of refurbished suites were arranged for the prime minister and some of his favourite objects and effects were brought down from London. A staff of over 100 accompanied him on board, including secretaries, typists, telegraphers and security guards.

The *Franconia* was restored for duties on Cunard's Canadian liner service until sold to the breakers in 1956. The *Carinthia* was not as fortunate. She became a war casualty, being torpedoed off the Irish coast by a Nazi submarine in June 1940.

The somewhat odd-fitting *Lancastria* was used for considerable cruising, often cheap-fare Depression voyages in the 1930s. One notable voyage was a six-night cruise out of Liverpool in May 1935 that included participation in the enormous Silver Jubilee review off Spithead for King George V. Cunard was officially represented by two larger liners, the *Berengaria* and *Homeric*.

The *Lancastria*, built at Glasgow in 1922, had one of the most tragic endings in all maritime history. Requisitioned as a trooper in September 1939, she was used for the evacuation of refugees from France in June 1940. On 17 September, she took on 5,000 escaping from the Nazi invasion forces and this included large numbers of women and children. Shortly afterwards, she was attacked by Nazi aircraft. The first bomb went through her funnel and exploded in the engine room, and the other two fell into the cargo holds and blew out the sides of the ship. Personal accounts were that the 578ft-long *Lancastria* seemed to 'jump out of the water'. The liner sank within twenty minutes with the loss of over 3,000, or perhaps over 4,000. The tragedy was horrific and so demoralising that Churchill ordered that the full details not be released until the end of the war, in 1945.

The six 'A-Class' Cunarders, built between 1922 and 1925, were smaller ships at just under 14,000 tons and much more functional in design as well as decoration. They were the *Antonia*, *Andania*, *Ausonia*, *Aurania*, *Alaunia* and *Ascania*. On board, there was a more evident divide between upper-deck cabin class and a far more austere third class. On board the *Antonia*, as an example, her capacity was for 1,706 passengers in all – 484 cabin class and 1,222 third class. A considerable cargo capacity supplemented their incomes. They were also ideal little Atlantic liners – they could be used on the New York run or to Boston or on the Canadian service. They could also run inexpensive cruises.

The Cunard careers of five of these ships were comparatively short, however. Only the 538ft-long *Ascania* returned to Cunard service after the war, going onto the Canada run but with reduced, post-war quarters of as few as 650 passengers. She was scrapped in 1956. Otherwise, the *Andania* was sunk by a German U-boat off Iceland in June 1940. Meanwhile, the remaining four were, due to wartime shortages of suitable tonnage, sold to the British Admiralty, stripped of their passenger quarters and rebuilt as fleet repair ships for the Royal Navy. The *Antonia* became HMS *Wayland* in 1944, and then was scrapped four years later in Scotland. The *Alaunia*, restyled as HMS *Alaunia*, finished her days at a scrapyard in Scotland in 1957. The *Ausonia*, serving the fleet for many years at Malta, was decommissioned in 1964 and broken up in Spain. By then, and nearly 45 years of age, she was the last of this group.

Often co-ordinated into Cunard Line's transatlantic schedules, Glasgow-based Anchor Line operated the three-funnel *Caledonia* and *Transylvania*. At just over 17,000 tons, they resembled mini superliners – each ship had three funnels. While the first and the third stacks were in fact dummies, the design made the ships seem larger. Anchor offered sailings between Glasgow and New York, often via Londonderry. The *Caledonia* had accommodation for as many as 1,408 passengers – 205 first class, 403

Festivity at sea! The *Lancastria* was painted in a more tropical, heat-resistant white in the 1930s. She is seen here docked at New York's Pier 90 with three of the *Aquitania*'s four funnels visible (Richard K. Morse Collection).

second class and 800 in low-fare third class. The ships also made cruises, including Depression-era 'long weekends' – four days from New York to Halifax for $45. Anchor also operated three single-stackers, each similar to the aforementioned Cunarders and named *California*, *Tuscania* and *Cameronia*. Anchor's passenger services on the Atlantic never reopened after the Second World War, however. The company decided to retain only its UK–India passenger operation, which endured until the mid-1960s.

Glasgow-based as well, the Donaldson Line added its largest passenger ships yet, the 13,400grt *Athenia* and *Letitia*, in 1923 and 1925 respectively. They were designed for the North Atlantic, trading between Glasgow and Montreal. Practical ships, they were intended to be unpretentious. Sunk on 3 September 1939, the *Athenia* gained a rather dubious ocean liner history: she was the first U-boat victim of the Second World War. The 523ft-long ship went down some 200 miles west of the Hebrides with the loss of 112. The second ship, the *Letitia*, survived the war – serving as an armed merchant cruiser, then a troopship and finally as a hospital ship for the Canadians. Taken over by the British Ministry of Transport after the war, she was renamed *Empire Brent* and in 1948 began carrying troops to and from the Far East. In 1950, she had added passengers: outward migrants to Australia and New Zealand. A later assignment was to carry Dutch nationals out of troubled Indonesia. Finally, the government of New Zealand chartered the ship (with Donaldson Line as managers) and had her refitted as a 1,088-berth, all-one-class migrant ship *Captain Cook*. She then entered regular service between Glasgow and Auckland via Panama. This schedule was only interrupted in the summer of 1955 when the ship was sub-chartered to operate seven voyages between Glasgow and Montreal, the very route she sailed in the 1920s and 1930s. In October 1959, the *Captain Cook* made her twenty-fifth and final sailing

outbound from Glasgow to New Zealand with a last load of 1,050 migrants. After a return stop at Malaya with returning troops, she was sold to scrap merchants at Inverkeithing.

Also for the Canadian trade, Canadian Pacific Steamships added three sisters: *Montcalm*, *Montrose* and *Montclare*. These 16,400grt sisters were created for service from Liverpool to Quebec City and Montreal in the ice-free months on the St Lawrence between April and December. In deep winter, they terminated their crossings at Saint John, New Brunswick. These ships were created especially for the westbound migrant trade, a fact reflected by their passenger configuration – 542 in cabin class and 1,268 in third class. Later, in 1928–29, Canadian Pacific wanted to step up its competitive place on

Departure for Liverpool! Cunard's smaller *Alaunia* departs from Pier 54 on an eight-night crossing to Liverpool. The date is 1930 (Richard Faber Collection).

Donaldson Line's *Athenia* ran crossings between Glasgow and Montreal, and later became the first passenger ship casualty of the Second World War (Richard Faber Collection).

A very basic passenger ship: Canadian Pacific's *Minnedosa* was intended for the Hamburg America Line but the First World War changed those plans. Instead, she joined Canadian Pacific. Sold to the Italians in 1935, she later became the troopship *Piemonte* for Mussolini's campaigns in Africa (Alex Duncan).

Organised seating: the cabin-class dining room aboard the 16,400grt *Montclare* of Canadian Pacific (Author's Collection).

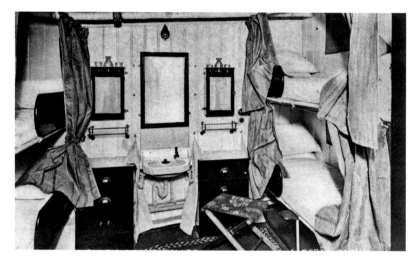

A four-berth cabin in third class aboard the 1,810-berth *Montclare* (Author's Collection).

The handsome, twin-funnel *Duchess of Atholl* is off on a cruise in this view from her maiden year, 1929. Sadly, she was torpedoed and sunk in the South Atlantic during the Second World War, in October 1942 (Alex Duncan).

the Canadian run with four very smart, good-looking sisters: the 20,100-ton *Duchess of Atholl*, *Duchess of Bedford*, *Duchess of Richmond* and *Duchess of York*. Built on the Clyde, they were in fact preludes to the company's biggest, finest and fastest liners for the Atlantic as well as the Pacific – the 42,000grt *Empress of Britain* and the 26,000grt *Empress of Japan*.

On the Atlantic and soon everywhere else, trading conditions changed drastically following the devastating Wall Street Crash in October 1929.

Even the most popular ships, such as Cunard's mighty *Aquitania* and White Star's popular *Majestic*, began to carry fewer and fewer passengers, even sailing half-full. The Atlantic slid into deepening decline – from 1 million travellers in 1930 to 500,000 five years later. Even the great Cunard Line, like many others, was forced to lay up ships. The ocean liner future was not bright, great caution and even reluctances were the orders of the day and, almost expectedly, there were some financial casualties.

3

TWO DUTCH SISTERS: THE *VEENDAM* AND *VOLENDAM*

The Holland America Line suffered considerable losses in the First World War. Typically, reconstruction and replacement were orders of the day. The New York service had priority, of course, and this included plans for a pair of 15,400grt sister ships. Dutch and other European immigrants would fill the third-class quarters on westbound crossings and that new, emerging wave of American tourists going to Europe would find accommodation as well. Holland America turned to Harland & Wolff, the noted shipbuilder, where a series of twin-funnel liners had been ordered by a consortium – Holland America, Hamburg America, North German Lloyd and Red Star Line. These ships had actually been ordered before the war, in 1914, but then postponed and finally the idea abandoned altogether. These were very practical ships –

neither large nor very fast and certainly not overly luxurious. They were not especially notable in any way, in fact.

The first of these ships for Holland America was the 572ft-long *Volendam*, which was built at Harland & Wolff's Govan yard in Scotland and was to be launched on 23 June 1922, but remained stuck in the slip. A second attempt also failed. Finally, the ship was launched two weeks later, on 6 July. Afterward, she was towed to Belfast and completed that November. The *Veendam*

The fine-looking, 24,149grt *Rotterdam*, completed in 1908, disembarks passengers along the Dalmatian coast during a long Mediterranean cruise (Alex Duncan).

Tense times! The *Volendam* is outbound from New York in September 1939 just as war is declared in Europe. She has been painted with vivid neutrality markings along her sides. She went on to become a valiant wartime troopship (Cronican-Arroyo Collection).

followed in May 1923. Used on the Rotterdam–New York run, the pair also did considerable cruising. Both survived the war intact and then resumed Holland America liner services. The *Volendam* was broken up in 1952, the *Veendam* a year later.

Holland America also ordered a quartet of passenger-cargo ships for its Northern Europe–Caribbean–Gulf of Mexico–New Orleans service in 1920–21. They were named *Edam*, *Leerdam*, *Maasdam* and *Spaarndam*. In addition to cargo, they each had a small first class as well as a larger, austere third class for westbound immigrants. Comfortable ships, the 8,900grt vessels were each given an extra funnel to make them seem larger and more liner-like. They were, however, victims of the Depression and missed voyages and were downgraded to ninety passengers each and lost that second

dummy funnel. The *Edam* and *Leerdam* survived the war and afterward appeared on the depleted Rotterdam–New York run before being scrapped in the mid-fifties.

Holland America's greatest attention was focused, however, on their new flagship. The initial *Statendam* was launched at Harland & Wolff's Belfast yard in 1914, but sat for several years incomplete and waiting. She was requisitioned by the British Government in 1917 for urgent troopship duties. To be managed by Cunard, her name was changed to *Justicia* but plans changed and White Star handled her operations. Her time was brief – she was torpedoed in the North Atlantic in July 1918. Holland America was without a flagship.

Soon after the war ended, the British Government offered compensation for the *Statendam* and other ships. Plans at Belfast were brought forward and modified slightly, but resulted in a long delayed construction process. The new 697ft-long liner was laid down in 1921, but then not launched until 1925. Delays followed and the 29,500-tonner was towed to Rotterdam in 1927 and then finally sailed to New York on her maiden voyage in April 1929. Affectionately dubbed 'Queen of the Spotless Fleet' (Holland America ships were noted especially for their immaculate condition), she was quickly established as a transatlantic favourite and remained very popular. Her decor, avoiding the growing trend toward the moderne that became Art Deco, was very traditional in tone: dark woods, stained glass, heavy chandeliers and furniture and thick, dark carpeting. 'The smoking room was so Dutch, it seemed to have been lifted out of Amsterdam,' remembered the late Everett Viez, an ocean liner historian and New York City-based travel agent. She had many other fine features: an array of suites in first class, a palm court, veranda cafe, fine dining room, Turkish bath, gymnasium and indoor swimming pool. Altogether, she could accommodate up to 1,280 passengers – 510 in first class, 344 second class and 426 third class.

The classic-looking, three-funnel *Statendam* also ran cruises: five nights to Bermuda, two and three weeks in the Caribbean and as long as eight weeks around the Mediterranean. Her fifty-eight-night cruise in 1935 was priced from $625 in first class and $340 in tourist class.

The *Statendam* had a very short life, however. She sailed for little more than ten years in Holland America service. During the Nazi invasion of Rotterdam, on 11 May 1940, the liner was bombed, caught in a crossfire and burned out. She smouldered for five days. In August, her wrecked hull was towed to a nearby scrapyard, dismantled and some metals, quite sadly, found their way into Nazi munitions factories.

From Belgium, the Red Star Line ran a transatlantic service between Antwerp and New York. They had the superb, three-funnel *Belgenland*, a 2,600-passenger ship dating from 1914–17, but which turned increasingly to cruising – including the likes of luxurious, five-month-long world cruises. Other noted ships included the 16,400grt sisters *Westernland* and *Pennland*.

Both Belfast built, the *Westernland* had been the Regina of Britain's Dominion Line and later sailed for White Star before passing to Red Star in 1929 (but retaining her British registry). She hoisted the German colours in 1935. The 2,400-berth *Pennland* had been ordered in 1913 for the American Line, but for intended British flag service. Her completion was delayed, however, by the war and instead the 600ft-long ship was finished as the *Pittsburgh* in 1922 for the White Star Line. She was transferred to Red Star in 1925 and renamed *Pennland* a year later. She too went under the German flag in 1935. Both the *Westernland* and *Pennland* were sold in 1939, just before the outbreak of the Second World War, to the Holland America Line. The *Westernland* was later sold to the British Ministry of Transport in 1942 and converted to a repair ship. While it was proposed to convert her into a whale factory ship in 1946, the plan never came to pass and instead she was sold to British ship-breakers. The *Pennland* was less fortunate. She was attacked by Nazi bombers while on a trooping voyage in the Gulf of Athens on 25 April 1941. Seven bombs exploded in the engine room, causing the hull to burst open. Most fortunately, only four lives were lost.

Classic style: Holland America Line opted to use a very traditional, three-funnel design for their new flagship, the 697ft-long *Statendam*, commissioned in 1929. She is seen here arriving at Boston, as part of an Atlantic crossing, on 16 July 1938 (Author's Collection).

4

GERMANY'S BIG FOUR

Following the devastation of the First World War, the resumption of passenger liner service represented a new beginning, a revival, a great restoration. The once large and powerful North German Lloyd, for example, which owned some of the largest and most luxurious liners, was reduced to owning a single freighter, the 800-ton *Grussgott*. By 1929, North German Lloyd had fifty ships. That same year, the company introduced the *Bremen*, which was not only one of the world's largest and most luxurious liners, but the fastest ship afloat. The Lloyd was rightfully proud.

The 1920s were primarily a period of replacement. Liners were, however, more moderate and medium sized. There was almost a caution in building very large ships at first. After all, trading conditions had changed. Most of all, the US Government greatly reduced the almost endless flow of immigrants onto its shores.

By the late twenties, enthusiasm peaked once again. A pair of intended 35,000-tonners that would be partnered with the highly successful *Columbus* were redesigned and emerged as 50,000-tonners – among the largest liners afloat. More importantly, the *Bremen* and *Europa* were the fastest – both Blue Riband champions.

At the war's end, the Germans, the Hamburg America Line, was allowed to keep the mechanically troubled *Victoria Luise*, a pre-war cruise ship that had been the Blue Riband champion *Deutschland*, a four-stacker dating from 1900. During the war, there had been plans to make the 684ft-long ship over as an armed merchant cruiser, but her mechanical problems stopped the project. Instead, she sat out the war years unused, rusting and in deepening neglect and decay. In 1919–20, it was decided to refit and reactivate the 16,333-tonner as a very basic immigrant ship, carrying a mere 36 in first class and as many as 1,350 in third class. Renamed *Hansa*, she was further demoded – two of her four funnels were removed and now she sailed with two stacks. She was used in the Hamburg–New York service (and later Hamburg–Halifax), but her days were numbered. She was sold to Hamburg scrappers in 1925.

Hamburg America was able to build new tonnage, but opted for large passenger-cargo liners. The 627ft-long *Albert Ballin*, named after the company's genius pre-war director, and her sister, the *Deutschland*, were very conservative ships with four masts that were reminders of the sailing ships of the prior century. The 20,815grt *Albert Ballin* was created to carry 1,551 passengers in three classes and six holds of freight. She and her sister were followed by two slightly different sisters, the *Hamburg* and *New York*, in 1926. The 'Big Four', as they were called, made weekly sailings between Hamburg and New York with stops at Southampton and Cherbourg in each direction. Successful ships, they were each re-engined in 1929–30 and then lengthened in 1933–34.

A pre-First World War speed champion and noted four-stacker, Hamburg America Line's *Deutschland*, and later *Victoria Luise*, was demoded after the war, in 1919–20, with two funnels and as the migrant ship *Hansa*. She is seen departing from New York's Pier 84 in 1922 (Author's Collection).

Using a very traditional, dated design of four masts, the *Albert Ballin* – but seen here as the renamed *Hansa* in 1936 – arrives in New York Harbor (Roger Scozzafava Collection).

In this aerial view dated September 1938, the 677ft-long *Hansa* departs from New York, sailing fifteen hours early and leaving her 350 passengers behind. She had been given very terse 'hurry home' orders by her Nazi-controlled owners since there was a growing possibility of war in Europe (Cronican-Arroyo Collection).

The 1,558-passenger *Deutschland* is seen just before her midnight sailing from New York's Pier 84 on 1 August 1935 (Cronican-Arroyo Collection).

Under pressure from the Nazi regime in 1935, the *Albert Ballin* was renamed *Hansa*. Ballin was Jewish. Largely unused during the Second World War, she was called to duty rather late, in 1945, becoming a training ship for the German Navy. She was, however, mined at Warnemünde that March. Salvaged by the Soviets in 1949, she was thoroughly rebuilt before resuming service as the *Sovetsky Sojus* in 1955. She was then the largest ship under the Soviet flag and was used mostly out in Far Eastern waters, sailing out of Vladivostok. Renamed *Soyuz* in 1980, she was scrapped a year later, then aged 58 years old.

The *Deutschland* was lost in the war. She was attacked by British aircraft in the Bay of Lübeck on 3 May 1945 and sunk. Her remains were raised three years later and scrapped. The slightly larger, 21,132grt *Hamburg* also found post-war life with the Soviets after the Second World War. Used as an accommodation ship by the Nazis from 1940, she struck a mine and sank on 7 March 1945 while evacuating forces from the Eastern Front. She was salvaged five years later, in 1950, by the Soviets and slowly restored. Intended to be a passenger liner, plans changed and, in 1960, she was completed as the whaling mother ship *Yuri Dolgoruki*. She endured until she was scrapped in 1977. Her sister, the *New York*, was another wartime casualty. She was hit by Allied bombers and sunk at Kiel on 3 April 1945. Her wreckage was salvaged in 1949 and then towed to England for scrapping.

Another important pair of post-war German liners were the near-sisters *Reliance* and *Resolute*. Rather impressive-looking three-stackers based on the design of the giant 1913-built *Imperator* (later Cunard's *Berengaria*), they were ordered in 1914 as the *William O'Swald* and *Johann Heinrich Burchard* for

Hamburg America emphasised its grand and golden history in promoting its liner services in the 1920s. This advertisement dates from 1928 (*National Geographic* magazine).

Hamburg America's second pair of new Atlantic liners, the *New York* (seen here off New York Harbor) and the *Hamburg*, had two instead of four masts (Cronican-Arroyo Collection).

Traditions make for Progress

Four great ocean liners, practically new and exceedingly popular, have been withdrawn from service. New engines are being installed to further increase their speed. The passenger accommodations remodelled to provide every element of luxury.

"The best is none too good", has been a Hamburg-American Line tradition for over 80 years, and accounts for the expenditure of millions of dollars for improvements on the ALBERT BALLIN, DEUTSCHLAND, HAMBURG and NEW YORK — the "*Famous Four*" of the Atlantic.

Seven days to Europe—moderate rates—vibrationless speed—remarkable steadiness due to special anti-rolling equipment —a sailing every Wednesday midnight.

This de luxe Express Service is supplemented by a popular Cabin Service, embracing the new motorships ST. LOUIS and MILWAUKEE, and the steamship CLEVELAND.

HAMBURG-AMERICAN
39 Broadway   LINE   New York
Branches in Chicago, Philadelphia, Boston, St. Louis, San Francisco, Los Angeles, Cleveland, Seattle, Montreal, Toronto, Winnipeg, Regina, Edmonton, or local steamship agents.

Skilful operation! Four tugs (one behind the ship) help dock the 677ft-long *Hamburg* at New York's Pier 84 in this view from 1935 (Cronican-Arroyo Collection).

Bound for Europe: the 17-knot *New York* heads for Cherbourg, Southampton and Hamburg (Author's Collection).

The bombed and battered remains of the *New York* as seen on 5 April 1949. She had been sunk in Allied attacks at Kiel (Cronican-Arroyo Collection).

Hamburg America Line's South Atlantic service, from Hamburg and other North European ports to Rio de Janeiro, Santos, Montevideo and Buenos Aires. The war changed everything, however, and their construction was slowed and then stopped. In the midst of the hostilities, in 1916, they were sold to the Dutch, to Royal Holland Lloyd, and finally completed in 1920 as the *Brabantia* and *Limburgia*. They were used, albeit very briefly, on the Amsterdam–East Coast of South America service. They were sold again, in 1922, to the newly created United American Line, renamed *Resolute* and *Reliance*, and moved onto the North Atlantic – sailing between Hamburg and New York. A year later, in 1923, and a reflection of American Prohibition laws, they were changed to the Panamanian flag, becoming two of the first ships to use a 'flag of convenience'. There were further changes in 1926 when the 615ft-long sisters were sold outright to Hamburg America, but retained their names. Both continued on the Atlantic, but turned to more and more cruising, becoming two of the most popular ships in leisure service. The *Reliance* burned out in Hamburg harbour in August 1938 and her twisted wreckage was scrapped three years later; the *Resolute* was sold to Italian scrappers in 1935, but then resold to the Mussolini government, renamed *Lombardia* and used to carry troops to East Africa. She was sunk in 1943, during the Allied bombing of Naples, and her remains scrapped three years later.

Similar to the aforementioned pair, the 16,900grt *Cleveland* and *Cincinnati* endured similar changes. Built in 1909 for Hamburg America service to New York, the ships were left in New York when the war started in August 1914, then seized by Americans in April 1917 and reactivated as US troopships – the *Cleveland* becoming the USS *Mobile*. Sold in 1920, she became the *King Alexander* for the London-based Byron Steamship Company for Mediterranean–New York service. She changed hands again, in 1923, going to the United American Lines and reverting to the name *Cleveland*. The 2,841-passenger ship was back on the North Atlantic, later returning to German colours, but then became an early victim of the Depression. She was laid up in 1931 and sold for scrap two years later. Her sister, the *Cincinnati*, which fell into American hands and became the USS *Covington*, was torpedoed and sunk in the North Atlantic in 1918.

Hamburg America's rival, the North German Lloyd, also had a slow but steady reawakening after the First World War. Most notably, two 32,500grt sisters were under construction, the sisters *Columbus* and *Hindenburg*, but then all work eventually stopped. The ships were unfinished when the war finally ended in November 1918. Afterward, the *Columbus* was ceded to the British as reparations and finished as the *Homeric* for service with the White Star Line. The intended *Hindenburg* was then renamed *Columbus*, but not launched for

North German Lloyd's *Berlin* at the Columbus Quay at Bremerhaven in 1925 (Cronican-Arroyo Collection).

almost four years, until August 1922. Another two years passed before the 775ft-long liner finally entered service to New York. She was Germany's largest, most luxurious liner and could accommodate 1,725 passengers in three classes.

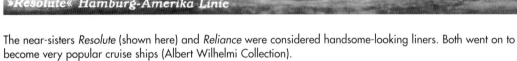

The near-sisters *Resolute* (shown here) and *Reliance* were considered handsome-looking liners. Both went on to become very popular cruise ships (Albert Wilhelmi Collection).

Caribbean waters! Passengers from the *Resolute* are tendered ashore during a three-week cruise to the West Indies in 1928 (Author's Collection).

Off on another long cruise! The 615ft-long *Reliance*, outbound from New York, caught fire and burned out at Hamburg on 7 August 1938. Her remains were scrapped three years later (Author's Collection).

The *Columbus* was nearly ruined, however, during a crossing in August 1927. The starboard shaft broke, which caused the machinery to race and nearly destroy itself. She was sent to a *Bremen* shipyard, fitted with a temporary engine (from the Lloyd freighter *Schwaben*) and then later fully repaired. In 1929, during a major refit, the *Columbus* was fitted with new engines, raising her service speed to as much as 23 knots. She was also fitted with low squat funnels. All this was done to become the third unit of the Lloyd's express run to New York, being teamed with new, far larger, much faster *Bremen* and *Europa*.

The *Columbus* was a very early casualty of the Second World War. When war was imminent in August 1939, she was on a cruise to the Caribbean, but was ordered to offload her American passengers at Havana and seek sanctuary itself at Vera Cruz. Almost four months later, in December, she was ordered back to Germany. She was stopped, however, off the Virginia coast and then, refusing surrender, the ship was deliberately set on fire and the sea cocks opened. She sank on 19 December in the western Atlantic. Her crew was rescued by an American warship.

North German Lloyd added smaller, intermediate liners during the 1920s. Among them was the 13,325grt *Munchen*, a 551ft-long ship completed in the summer of 1923. She survived a fire at her New York City pier in February 1930 and then went on to become the refitted cruise ship *General von Steuben* (a name later modified to *Steuben*). She had an especially tragic ending during the war, however. Used as a moored accommodation ship until 1944, she was revived for active service to carry wounded soldiers to Germany from Baltic

Above: Grandeur at sea! The high ceilings in the first-class main lounge aboard the *Columbus* (Hapag-Lloyd).

Left: Grand revival! The completion of the 32,581grt, 1,725-passenger *Columbus* in 1924 was the most significant sign of North German Lloyd's revival following the German fleet's destruction and the devastation of the First World War. The 775ft liner was said to be a hint of bigger, better ships to come. She was rebuilt in 1929 with squat funnels so as to better resemble the brand new 50,000grt *Europa* and *Bremen* (Cronican-Arroyo Collection).

Sailing to the sun! Seen tendering at La Guaira in Venezuela in 1938, the *Columbus* did considerable cruising. She had an outdoor pool positioned between her twin funnels (Hapag-Lloyd).

Luxurious evenings! Another view of the main lounge (Hapag-Lloyd).

Homeport waters! The *Milwaukee* at the landing stage at Hamburg (Hapag-Lloyd).

Warm-weather days! Repainted in tropical white, the *Milwaukee* later did a considerable amount of cruising and was specially advertised as a 'floating health spa' (Author's Collection).

ports. On 9 February 1945, while bound for Kiel, she had 2,500 wounded, 2,000 refugees and 450 crew on board when she was struck by two torpedoes fired by a Soviet sub. She sank quickly while over 3,000 perished.

Another Lloyd liner was the 15,286grt *Berlin*, which was built at *Bremen* in 1925. She made history in her second life, however. Mined and sunk off Swinemünde on 1 February 1945, she was salvaged by the Soviets in 1949 and returned to passenger service eight years later, in 1957, as the *Admiral Nakhimov*. Used mostly in Black Sea service out of Odessa, she was rammed by a Soviet cargo vessel on 31 August 1986 and quickly sank. Some 423 passengers and crew perished. It was the worst peacetime disaster in Soviet maritime history.

Hamburg America continued to reinforce its transatlantic service and, in 1929, added the 16,700-ton sisters *Milwaukee* and *St Louis*. American names were used in hopes of attracting more passengers – Germans going to America and German-Americans returning to the homeland. Both ships,

with almost 1,000 berths divided between three classes, also did considerable cruising. The 575ft-long *Milwaukee* was in fact repainted in all white and restyled as a 'floating health spa'. The *Milwaukee* survived the war only to be allocated to the British in 1945, but then burnt a year later. Her remains were soon scrapped. The *St Louis* made headlines when, in May–June 1939 and with 900 Jewish refugees on board, she was denied landing rights in Cuba and then in America. The sailing, later dubbed 'Voyage of the Damned', was a sinister propaganda effort by the Nazis to prove the undesirability of Jews. The passengers were returned to Europe, disembarked at Antwerp and later divided among four nations. The 16-knot *St Louis* fled from New York in August 1939 as war was imminent, returned to Germany, and sat idle for most of the war years only to be bombed during an Allied air raid on Kiel in August 1944. Her partly damaged remains were used after the war, however. She was a temporary hotel at Hamburg from 1946 until 1950. The *St Louis* was scrapped two years later.

5

DISTANT WATERS: EAST OF SUEZ

After the First World War, P&O – the legendary British shipping company more exactly titled the Peninsular & Oriental Steam Navigation Company Limited – was riding high. Alone, they added their biggest ships yet: the 20,800grt sisters *Mooltan* and *Maloja*. Their splendid *Viceroy of India*, of similar size, was added in 1928. The war had disrupted their new ship construction programme. Timetables, projections and introductions for new ships were greatly disrupted.

The company's largest liners yet for London–Suez–Sydney service, the 15,800grt *Naldera* and her near-sister *Narkunda*, were delayed at the shipbuilders. Warships had priority. The former was being built on the Clyde, the construction of the latter at Belfast. Both ships had been laid down in 1914, but sat – their hulls left untouched. By 1917, there was some rethinking – there were plans for them as armed merchant cruisers, then as cargo ships and then as hospital ships. Then plans developed to complete them as troopships, but then there were other ideas to completely redesign them as aircraft carriers. The 605ft-long *Naldera* was actually launched in December 1917, but then was laid up for another two years. A proud-looking three-stacker, she finally entered Australian service in April 1920. The *Narkunda* followed her within weeks.

Quickly, the two ships were known for their high comforts. The first-class dining room on board rose three decks in height and created better ventilation in often sweltering voyages through the Mediterranean, the Suez, the Red Sea and across the Indian Ocean. The ships' interiors often reached over 100 degrees. The amenities even extended to second class – there were two ceiling fans in the more expensive double-bedded staterooms. On board the *Narkunda*, her full capacity for 673 was divided between 426 in first class and 247 in second class. A first-class passage cost $200 in the mid-twenties for the forty-two-day voyage from London to Sydney via Marseilles, Port Said, Aden, Bombay, Colombo, Fremantle, Adelaide and Melbourne.

East of Suez! The 16,118grt *Narkunda* and her near-sister *Naldera* were P&O's largest and finest liners in the very early twenties. They were used on the London–Bombay as well as London–Sydney services (V.H. Young & L.A. Sawyer Collection).

Later used on the London–Bombay express run, the *Naldera* saw only eighteen years of P&O service when she went to the breakers in 1938; the *Narkunda* was sunk off North Africa in November 1942.

Built at Belfast in 1923, the 20,000grt sisters *Mooltan* and *Maloja* were the largest P&O liners to date. Fitted only with a foremast as well as twin all-black funnels, they carried considerable freight and comparatively few passengers – 327 in first class and 329 in second class. Used on the London–Suez–Australia run, both survived the Second World War, but (and like several other pre-war P&O passenger ships) were downgraded as pure migrant ships but still on the Australian run.

Luxury on the eastern run! The first-class music room aboard the 673-berth *Narkunda* as seen in this 1920 photograph (P&O).

Ships such as the medium-sized 16,200grt *Moldavia* of P&O were given a second dummy smokestack so as to appear larger, safer and more reliable (P&O).

Right: The age of empire and the so-called 'Empire Builders' very much supported ships such as P&O's *Chitral*, seen here at Singapore in a view from 1933. The *Chitral* was assigned to P&O's Far Eastern service – sailing from London to Singapore, Hong Kong and Japan (P&O).

The low-fare migrant run to Australia also interested P&O, and for this the company built five 13,000grt ships in 1921–22. Named *Ballarat, Baradine, Balranald, Barrabol* and *Bendigol*, they were very austere ships, carrying 490 in third class and 700 in even less-expensive steerage.

In 1922–23, to strengthen their colonial run to Bombay, P&O added the 16,200grt sisters *Moldavia* and *Mongolia*. Practical twin-stackers that carried 400 passengers each and lots of freight, the *Mongolia* went on to give long service – becoming the *Rimutaka, Europa, Nassau* and *Acapulco* – before being scrapped in 1964–65.

P&O also built a quartet of 'express steamers' for the very important Indian colonial service named *Ranpura, Ranchi, Rawalpindi* and *Rajputana*. They sailed regularly from London and from Southampton the following day for Gibraltar, Marseilles (a popular alternative for passengers wanting to avoid the notorious Bay of Biscay and instead use the train from London, across France and also thereby cutting a week's time off the voyage), then Malta, Port Said, a transit of the Suez Canal, Aden and finally Bombay. Later, in the 1930s, these ships extended their run to the Far East – going beyond Bombay to Penang, Singapore, Hong Kong, Shanghai, Kobe and turnaround at Yokohama. The twenty-night voyage from London to Bombay was priced from £50 in the mid-twenties. Built by Harland & Wolff, the 16,619grt *Rawalpindi* carried 600 passengers: 310 in first class and 290 in second class.

P&O designers were pleased with the basic design of the *Ranchi* and her four sisters and created larger, even more luxurious ships: a trio for the London–Australia run named *Cathay, Comorin* and *Chitral*, and then onto a larger, faster, far grander ship – the 19,500grt *Viceroy of India*. Launched in September 1928 from the yard of Alexander Stephen & Sons Limited of Glasgow, she was to have been named *Taj Mahal*, but entered service on the London–Bombay run in the winter of 1929 as the *Viceroy of India*. Quickly, she established a loyal following and was dubbed the premier British liner on the Indian colonial run. Quarters aboard the 612ft-long liner were arranged for 673 passengers – 415 in first class and 258 in second. Her decor reflected British life and style, ideas based on, say, a London club and country house in the English countryside. 'You are almost back in England when you step aboard at Bombay', read one brochure. Her decorative style meant antiques, paintings, dark woods, fireplaces and the inevitable Indian and Persian carpets. The 19-knot ship also became a popular cruise ship, especially in the Depression-era 1930s, with summer season voyages to Norway and the northern cities. She also cruised to the Canaries, West Africa, Spain, Portugal and to ports in the Mediterranean. A 'one-of-a-kind' in the large P&O fleet, she was noted for her rather unique turboelectric drive.

P&O's celebrated 19,500grt *Viceroy of India*, used on the London–Bombay run as well as for cruises, could carry 673 passengers – 415 in first class and 258 in second class (P&O).

Comfort on the Indian Ocean! The first-class dining room aboard P&O's *Rajputana*, a 16,568-tonner that was built in 1925 and used on the important London–Bombay route (P&O).

Long, leisurely afternoons! A portion of the first-class smoking saloon aboard the 595-passenger *Rajputana* (P&O).

Creature comforts! The outdoor pool on board the *Viceroy of India* (P&O).

In the wake of P&O's massive reconstruction and growth in the passenger ship business, another London-based company, the Orient Line added no less than five 20,000-tonners for the London–Sydney run. These ships were named *Orama*, *Oronsay*, *Otranto*, *Orford* and *Orontes*. They were a blend of traditional exteriors, each having two thin funnels, and classical interiors.

The Australian Government even dabbled in the busy, lucrative migrant trade between London, Fremantle, Melbourne and Sydney. In 1921–23, they created five 13,850grt, one-class ships: *Moreton Bay*, *Largs Bay*, *Hobsons Bay*, *Esperance Bay* and *Jervis Bay*. They were not successful, however, were beset with labour problems and by 1928 were sold to the White Star Line and then sold again, in 1933, to the London-based Aberdeen & Commonwealth Line, a joint venture of P&O and the Shaw Savill Line.

Another great 'arm of the British Empire' was British India or BI – the British India Steam Navigation Company Limited. This London-headquartered firm was vast in scope, trading not only between London and East Africa, but East Africa to India, India to Southeast Asia and the Far East, India to Australia and from London out to the Far East. Combination passenger-cargo ships featured strongly in their planning. There were no less than seventeen sisters and near-sisters of BI's 'M-Class' – ships such as

the 9,100grt *Mulbera*. The 483-footer carried 158 passengers (78 first class, 80 second class) and lots of cargo. She was used on the East African run – London to Marseilles, Port Said, Port Sudan, Aden, Mombasa and Beira. London to Beira took thirty-five days. Otherwise, these 'M-Class' were used on an Indian service – London to Tangier, Malta, Port Said, Suez, Aden, Colombo, Madras and turnaround at Calcutta. London to Calcutta was a run of thirty days.

Among others ships, British India introduced two notable passenger vessels in 1926, the 8,600grt sisters *Rohna* and *Rajula*. Built on the Clyde, they would see little of home waters for they were created for eastern service, the route between Madras and Singapore. Fitted with steam triple expansion engines, they were rather slow, making only 13 knots at top speed. Very functional ships with cargo space as well, they carried 180 passengers in cabin quarters and up to 5,000 in their 'tween decks. As deep-sea passenger ships, they were listed as having the highest capacities of their time, even exceeding the largest Atlantic superliners.

Both ships were called to war service. The *Rajula* served in eastern waters as a so-called 'hospital transport' while the *Rohna* was sent to the Mediterranean. She took on 2,000 American troops at Oran after which,

Basic style! The no-nonsense, no-frills look of the *Esperance Bay*, a migrant ship belonging to the Aberdeen & Commonwealth Line (Richard Faber Collection).

Carrying nearly 5,200 passengers each, the sisters *Rajula* (seen here) and *Rohna* had the highest passenger capacities of their time. Owned by the British India Steam Navigation Company Limited, they sailed between eastern India and Southeast Asia (P&O).

on 26 November 1943, she was attacked by a single Nazi aircraft, which was seen to release a radio-controlled glider bomb. This new weapon hit the 488ft-long *Rohna* near the aft end of the engine room, causing extensive fires to break out along the port side and allowing only the starboard side boats to be lowered. Many of these were swamped as soon as they left the ship because of the larger number of troops that had jumped overboard. Although the *Rohna* remained afloat for over an hour, the stern eventually settled to such a degree that the machinery broke loose and crashed through the hull, causing the ship to go down. In all, over 1,000 troops and 120 crew were lost in the incident, which ranked as the first sinking of a merchant vessel by a guided missile in history.

The *Rajula* resumed Indian passenger service in 1946 and served for another twenty-seven years before, in 1973, being sold to Indian buyers and becoming the Rangat. The 48-year-old ship sailed for another year before being broken up in India in 1974.

Another British firm, the Ellerman Lines, invested in the UK–India trade (as well as the UK–Africa trade) with profitable combination passenger-cargo ships such as the 330-passenger *City of Nagpur*.

Also using the Suez route on its East African and Around Africa services, Britain's Union-Castle had also lost tonnage in the First World War and so needed to rebuild and strengthen its post-war services. The company was constructing its largest liners yet just as the war started, but their construction was halted. Instead, they were commissioned as new post-war liners – the 18,900grt sisters *Arundel Castle* and *Windsor Castle*. They were created

especially for the all-important Mail Service to the South African Cape – from Southampton via Madeira or Las Palmas to Cape Town, Port Elizabeth, East London and Durban. Impressive ships at 661ft in length, each had four funnels and were in fact the last liners to have four stacks, as well as the only passenger ships away from the Atlantic to have as many. Both ships were, however, rebuilt in 1937 with a more modern pair of funnels. After that, Cunard's *Aquitania* was the last remaining four-stacker.

This pair was soon followed at Union-Castle by more modern ships, including the squat-funnel motor liners *Carnarvon Castle*, *Winchester Castle*

and *Warwick Castle*. Each 20,000 tons, they were the largest and finest mail ships of their day.

The London-based New Zealand Shipping Company ran a long-haul passenger and cargo service out to Auckland and Wellington, but via Curacao and the Panama Canal. In 1925, the company ordered its largest and finest ships yet: 16,700grt combination passenger-cargo liners named *Rangitiki*, *Rangitata* and *Rangitane*. They had three-class passenger quarters (for just under 600 passengers) and sizeable refrigerated spaces in their cargo areas for the homeward loads of New Zealand meats. Built on the Clyde, the construction of these 553ft-long ships was delayed, however, by three years. In that time, these intended single-stackers were redesigned with twin funnels so as to resemble larger ocean liners and create the illusion of greater size. While the *Rangitane* was lost during the Second World War, the *Rangitiki* and *Rangitata* went on to sail until the early 1960s. At the time of her final voyage, it was determined that the *Rangitata* had passed through the Panama Canal 144 times.

France's Messageries Maritimes looked after the colonial passenger, freight and mail from Marseilles out to Indochina. Rather expectedly, these ships were guaranteed full loads of passengers and large amounts of freight. This service was strengthened with new ships in the 1920s: the 14,600grt *Aramis* and the 10,000grt sisters *Compiègne* and *Fontainebleau*. Still larger, the 15,100grt sisters *D'Artagnan* and *Athos II* were added in 1924–25. Messageries Maritimes also looked after more local passenger services, such as Marseilles to Alexandria and Beirut, and for this they created the sisters *Champollion* and *Mariette Pacha*.

Combination passenger-cargo ships, such as Ellerman Lines' 9,654-ton *City of Exeter*, were popular as well as practical on such long-haul services as India, the Far East and New Zealand (Ellerman Lines).

Scenic setting! Given a second dummy funnel to appear more impressive, New Zealand Shipping Company's *Rangitiki* carried passengers as well as considerable cargo. This view, in New Zealand waters, dates from 1956 (Gillespie-Faber Collection).

Used on the Amsterdam–East Indies routes, the 14,642grt *Pieter Corneliszoon Hooft* belonged to the Nederland Line (Gillespie-Faber Collection).

Moderne style! Looking sleek and racy, Nederland Line's *Christiaan Huygens*, completed in 1928, was topped by a small, very simple, paint can-like funnel. The 570ft-long ship is seen here departing from Genoa, a port of call on her long voyages from Amsterdam out to Batavia (Richard Faber Collection).

Right: German Africa Line's *Usaramo* at Hamburg with the *Monte Rosa* of the Hamburg South America Line in the background (Gillespie-Faber Collection).

Also away from the North Atlantic services of the famed Holland America Line, Dutch shipowners maintained numerous services to other parts of the world – to the Caribbean, to the East Coast of South America, to South and East Africa and out to the colonial Dutch East Indies. On the latter service, the dominant players were the Nederland Line and the Rotterdam Lloyd. These firms built a succession of passenger-cargo ships for tropical service, one catering to government officials, teachers, traders, merchants, missionaries and colonial families. The 9,900grt *Patria* was one of the largest ships on this run, ordered in 1914, delayed and then commissioned in 1919. She had space for 332 passengers – 120 first class, 124 second class, 44 third class, 44 fourth class. She was routed from Rotterdam and Southampton to Lisbon, Gibraltar, Marseilles, Port Said, Colombo, Sabang, Belawan, Deli, Singapore and Batavia (Jakarta). These long voyages were eased somewhat by 1927 when a twenty-two-hour train service began between Rotterdam and Marseilles. This could replace five full days at sea. When the Depression set in by the 1930s, the Dutch sensibly offered alternate holiday voyages such as Rotterdam to Lisbon as short, escapist vacations. The 480ft-long *Patria* was sold off to the Soviets in 1934, renamed *Svir*, sunk at Leningrad during the Second World War, salvaged and then sailed until 1979, a career spanning fifty-nine years.

The Dutch also added the likes of the 10,300grt *Johan de Witt* and other passenger-cargo types such as the *Slamat* (1924), *Indrapoera* (1925), the larger *Pieter Corneliszoon Hooft* (1927) and finally the *Sibajak* (1928).

The 15,637grt *Christiaan Huygens* was one of the largest and finest liners on the Dutch East Indies trade. The 570ft-long ship was completed in the winter of 1928 for the Nederland Line. She had a rather novel design – to appear larger and of course longer, she was fitted with one, very small, almost paint can-like funnel. This also gave her a low, racy appearance. It also allowed for a greater amount of open-air deck space, a highly desirable amenity considering her long, often sweltering passages in the Red Sea and Indian Ocean. Carrying 572 passengers (269 first class, 250 second class and 53 third class), she was a very popular ship. She all but survived the Second World War, but then less than two weeks after VJ Day, and on a short voyage from Antwerp to Rotterdam, she struck an uncharted mine off the Dutch coast. Beached but badly damaged, she later broke in half and had to be scrapped.

To support its colonial holdings in the East, the Dutch created a vast group of small-sized passenger ships. The largest of these were the 10,900grt sisters *Nieuw Holland* and *Nieuw Zeeland*. Each carried 173 passengers divided

Serving the African colonies: Compagnie Maritime Belge's *Leopoldville* was used in government-supported service between Antwerp and the Belgian Congo (Cronican-Arroyo Collection).

between 123 in first class and 50 in third class. Built at Amsterdam and with a design that included twin funnels, the pair was used in service between Southeast Asia, colonial Java and Australian ports – Singapore to Batavia, Semerang, Surabaya, Brisbane, Sydney, Melbourne and Adelaide. They were long voyages – Singapore all the way to Adelaide took twenty-eight days. Operated by the KPM Line, based in Batavia, the *Nieuw Zeeland* was lost in the Second World War while the 527ft-long *Nieuw Holland* returned to service in the late 1940s but for the reorganised Royal Interocean Lines, another Dutch company. She sailed for thirty years until scrapped in 1959.

6

THE ITALIANS: WARM WATERS, LIDO DECKS AND HYPER DECOR

Italian passenger ships were rather small, largely geared for westbound migrants, and all but unnoticed prior to the First World War. Expansion and enlargement were in the wind soon afterward, however. Lloyd Sabaudo, one of the most prominent passenger lines, turned to experienced Glasgow shipbuilders, William Beardmore & Company Limited, for the construction of twin 18,700grt liners. Actually, there was an earlier start – an intended liner, the *Conte Rosso*, was launched at Glasgow in December 1917, but was commandeered for the war effort by the Royal Navy and completed as the aircraft carrier HMS *Argus*. Undaunted, however, Lloyd Sabaudo launched a new second *Conte Rosso* in the winter of 1921. She was followed by a twin

sister, the *Conte Verde*, launched in October 1921. Both splendid twin-stackers with quarters for up to 2,400 passengers including a very large third class for westbound migrants, the twin, 18½-knot liners rotated between Genoa–New York and Genoa–Rio de Janeiro–Buenos Aires services. Later, in 1932, and after the integration of Italian passenger companies to create the more effective Italian Line, both ships were assigned to the Far East run – sailing from Genoa and Naples to Port Said, Bombay, Colombo, Singapore, Manila and Shanghai – for another Italian firm, Lloyd Triestino. The *Conte Verde* was very nearly lost, in fact, when she was grounded during a typhoon near Hong Kong in September 1937. Badly damaged, she was only freed and refloated with great difficulty.

Far left: Sailing off! The 18,800grt *Conte Verde* sails past the Lower Manhattan skyline, with the Woolworth and Singer buildings in the background, off on a crossing to the Mediterranean (Cronican-Arroyo Collection).

Left: More exotic ports! Later used on the Italy–Far East run, the *Conte Verde* – then sailing for Lloyd Triestino – is seen at Shanghai in this photo from 1935 (Paolo Piccione Collection).

Like so many passenger ships of this era, the fates of these two liners ended with the Second World War. The 559ft-long *Conte Rosso* became a troopship in Mussolini's navy in 1940. But her days were numbered. On 24 May 1941, and while carrying 2,500 soldiers, she was torpedoed by a British submarine while in an otherwise heavily protected convoy bound for Tripoli. She sank 15 miles off the Sicilian coast with over 800 casualties. Meanwhile, the *Conte Verde* was interned in Shanghai in 1940 after Italy entered the war. In 1942, she was used by the Japanese for prisoner-of-war exchange voyages to and from China. A year later, after the fall of Mussolini's regime, the ship's Italian crew sabotaged and sank the liner to avoid Japanese capture. The Japanese Navy had her salvaged, repaired for trooping, but then only to be sunk during an American air raid on Maizuru in 1944. Her remains were raised in 1949 and then scrapped two years later.

Another Italian liner company was NGI, Navigazione Generale Italiana, and they built Italy's biggest and finest liners to date, the sister ships *Duilio* and *Giulio Cesare*. Constructed by the Ansaldo shipyard at Genoa, the 24,281grt *Duilio* and her sister divided their time between the New York and the East Coast of South American runs from Genoa. Noted for their ornate, heavily wood-panelled interiors, they were a prelude to subsequent Italian liners of the 1920s. When the Italian Line was created in 1932, both ships were transferred to the Italy–South Africa run under the banner of Lloyd Triestino. Sadly, they too were war losses – the *Duilio* was destroyed in an Allied air raid on Trieste in July 1944; the *Giulio Cesare*'s days ended at the same port, but during another Allied raid two months later. Their remains were scrapped in the late forties.

Unquestionably, two of the grandest and most ornate as well as most popular and long-serving of the Italian liners of this period were the near-sisters *Conte Biancamano* and *Conte Grande*. The 24,416grt *Conte Biancamano* was built in 1925 by William Beardmore at Glasgow; the 25,661grt *Conte Grande* was constructed two years later by Stabilimento Tecnico shipyard at Trieste. Both ships were built for Lloyd Sabaudo and were successors to the earlier *Conte Rosso* and *Conte Verde*. Expectedly, they had sizeable passenger accommodations such as aboard the 653ft-long *Conte Biancamano* being for 1,750 at capacity (280 first class, 420 second class, 390 third class, 660 fourth class). The decor on these ships was sometimes described as 'hyper Italian' – it was often a collection of styles that was 'busy' to mind as well as eye. On board the 19-knot *Conte Grande*, there were touches of Italian palacio, Mogul Indian, Arabian Nights and American cinema – and sometimes all used together. The general public saw it all as 'Italian, typically rich and typically gilded'. There were other touches as well, such as the Japanese-themed indoor pool aboard the *Conte Grande*.

Both ships survived the Second World War, serving as the American-operated USS *Hermitage* and USS *Monticello* respectively. Fortunately, they were returned to the Italians in 1947, but rebuilt with modern, post-war interiors. That extraordinary, pre-war decor was gone. Having long, useful lives, both ships endured until the early 1960s.

The two biggest, fastest and probably grandest Italian entries of the twenties were the 32,600grt sisters *Roma* and *Augustus*. They were the prime, highly successful express liners of their day on the Mediterranean–New York run. 'The *Roma* and *Augustus* were ornate, richly decorated ships,' said the late passenger ship historian Everett Viez. 'They were like floating palaces, even castles. They were so rich in their gilded Baroque stylings that they made a lasting impression on everyone who saw them. They were the ultimate Italian liners of their day.'

Classic passenger design! The good-looking *Giulio Cesare* departs from Genoa (Maurizio Eliseo Collection).

When commissioned in 1925, the 24,416grt *Conte Biancamano* was Italy's largest liner to date. She could carry 1,750 passengers in four classes (Author's Collection).

Sailing day! Lloyd Sabaudo's *Conte Biancamano* departs from New York's Pier 95 in this view, dated 1928 (Author's Collection).

Built by the Ansaldo shipyard at Sestri Ponente, near Genoa, they were commissioned a year apart – the *Roma* in September 1926, the *Augustus* in November 1927. The *Roma*'s first-class dining room was styled after an eighteenth-century palazzo and was capped by a great domed ceiling; the *Augustus* had a Japanese grill room for private dinner parties. In her vast quarters that included the novelty of a lido deck and outdoor swimming pool, the 711ft-long *Augustus* carried as many as 2,200 passengers in three classes. Also integrated into the new Italian Line in 1932, they also ran sailings to the East Coast of South America, short cruises from New York and long, more luxurious forty- to forty-five-day trips around the Mediterranean.

In 1939, there were rather big plans to rebuild these ships – with more powerful diesels and modernised with single funnels. The war interrupted these and instead they were converted to aircraft carriers for Mussolini's Navy. The *Roma* became *Aquila*; the *Augustus* changed to *Sparviero*. They were never put to use, however, and were then destroyed after the Italian capitulation in September 1944. In ruins, both ships were later scrapped.

The Cosulich Line added the splendid, 23,900-ton sisters *Saturnia* and *Vulcania* in 1927–28. They were introduced in February and December 1928, then joined Italian Line schedules in 1932 (but while Cosulich itself remained quite separate until 1937). 'They were two of the most charming liners ever to sail the Atlantic,' recalled Everett Viez:

Dazzling style! The cinema-afloat style as seen in this view of the first-class grand hall aboard the *Conte Grande,* dated 1927 (Author's Collection).

At first, we discounted them because of their stump, flat funnels. But on the inside, they were Italian Baroque to the hilt. They were cathedrals gone to sea! On board the *Vulcania*, the smoking room suggested Sir Francis Drake and the Spanish Armada. Then there were highly polished woods, gilded chandeliers and lamps, grand stairwells and an indoor pool of fine marbles and mosaics with adjoining steam baths, small bar and visitors' gallery. Every inch, they were grandeur – Italian grandeur, even Roman grandeur. Historically, this pair introduced the private veranda. Today, on cruise liners, it is very popular as a terrace or balcony. But on the *Saturnia* and *Vulcania*, there was an entire deck, and every first-class cabin along both sides had a private veranda. This was the very first time for such a feature. These verandas made these ships top draws in the travel industry. Of course, they were also favoured for their exceptional Italian cuisine and for their superb Cosulich service. They were two of the best-run liners of all time.

'The *Saturnia* and *Vulcania* were probably the most successful ships that Italian Line ever owned,' added the late Captain Mario Vespa, who worked for Cosulich Line in the 1930s:

They were successful before the war, but even more so afterward, in the late 1940s and in the '50s. Tens of thousands of Italian and European immigrants used them after the Second World War for their voyages to North America,

Repainted in the new, co-ordinated Italian Line colours, the 653ft-long *Conte Biancamano* is seen departing from Genoa in this 1932 view (Maurizio Eliseo Collection).

After extensive service as the American troopship USS *Hermitage,* the *Conte Biancamano* was restored, modernised and repainted with an all-white hull. She is seen here at Naples with the American liner *Independence* in the background (Maurizio Eliseo Collection).

Hyper-electric decor! The extraordinary first-class dining room aboard the 25,661grt *Conte Grande*. She was used in Mediterranean–New York service as well as on sailings to the east coast of South America (Author's Collection).

to Halifax and to New York. They were strong and solid – and excellent 'sea boats'. They sailed for Italian Line for an exceptional thirty-seven years.

Both ships fell into American hands after the Italian surrender in 1943 – the *Saturnia* becoming the hospital ship *Francis Y. Slanger*, while the *Vulcania* became a troopship. Returned to the Italians in late 1946, they were restored for Mediterranean–New York service and used until 1965. While the *Saturnia* went to the breakers, the *Vulcania* found further life with other Italians, the Siosa Lines, as the *Caribia*. Used in Europe–Caribbean service and later in Mediterranean cruising, she went aground at Cannes in September 1972, was badly damaged and too old to repair. Sold to Italian breakers, she was resold to Spanish breakers and then resold again, to Taiwanese scrappers. Towed out to the Far East, she was awaiting a berth at Kaohsiung, but then sprang leaks and began to flood. Later pumped out, the 631ft-long ship was finally towed to shore and demolished.

Biggest yet! The 32,600-ton *Roma* and her sister *Augustus* were Italy's largest, finest and fastest liners by the late twenties. Both were made over as aircraft carriers during the Second World War, but never saw service and were ultimately destroyed (Richard Faber Collection).

Busy day! The *Roma* is in the centre of this gathering of ships at Genoa. The *Conte Biancamano* and the *Conte Verde* are to the left (Richard Faber Collection).

126 - GENOVA - PANORAMA

BERENGARIA

The mighty *Berengaria*, one of the most popular Atlantic liners of all time (Author's Collection).

CUNARD LINE

There was great prestige in sailing with Cunard (Author's Collection).

CUNARD LINE

Prochains départs de
CHERBOURG pour NEW-YORK

MAURETANIA - 5 Fév.
AQUITANIA - 19 ..
BERENGARIA - 26 ..
AQUITANIA - 12 Mars

Durée Moyenne de la Traversée : 5 Jours, 8 Heures
SERVICE LE PLUS RAPIDE DU MONDE

Départ de New-York pour le Havre, le 12 Février

CUNARD LINE

MAURETANIA · BERENGARIA · AQUITANIA

FASTEST
OCEAN SERVICE
IN THE WORLD

SOUTHAMPTON · CHERBOURG
· NEW YORK ·

Cunard promoted its liner services from France, namely on the express run to and from Cherbourg (Author's Collection).

Cunard's 'Big Three' – the *Mauretania*, *Berengaria* and *Aquitania* (Author's Collection).

Above: A promotion in great poster art for Cunard's transocean service to and from Canada (Author's Collection).

Above right: A painting of the great *Berengaria* arriving at New York, by American artist Joseph Wilhelm (Author's Collection).

Right: Artist Tony Westmore's superb painting of the 919ft-long *Berengaria* docking at Southampton (Tony Westmore Collection).

The late Joseph Wilhelm's splendid painting of the glorious *Aquitania* (Author's Collection).

The Ocean Dock at Southampton by artist Stephen Card – showing the *Leviathan*, *Majestic* and *Berengaria* (Stephen Card Collection).

Looking far bigger than reality, the 13,000-ton *President Roosevelt* of the United States Lines seems to dominate the seas (Author's Collection).

Dutch style: the smoking room aboard the *Statendam* of 1929 (Holland America Line).

More interiors of the *Statendam* (Holland America Line).

The *Statendam* was one of the very last liners to not use Art Deco styling (Holland America Line).

Crossing on the Hamburg America Line, which was co-ordinated with United American Lines (Author's Collection).

Japanese artist Hayao Nogami's fine depiction of the *Kungsholm* of 1928 (Hayao Nogami Collection).

White Star's *Laurentic* of 1927 (Author's Collection).

SVENSKA AMERIKA LINIEN

Left: A striking poster of Sweden's *Kungsholm* (Author's Collection).

Artist Kenneth Shoesmith's superb depiction of Cunard's *Scythia* outbound from New York (Richard Faber Collection).

One of Cunard's 'A-Class', the *Ascania,* is shown passing the Bar lightship (Author's Collection).

Poster promotion of the Cunard service from Glasgow to Boston and New York (Author's Collection).

An interesting sketch of the *Samaria* (Author's Collection).

Above: Hamburg America Line's 'Big Four' service between Hamburg, Channel ports and New York (Author's Collection).

Top right: Another view of the 20,000-ton *Scythia* (Author's Collection).

Right centre: Off to the exotic East: Blue Funnel's 14,682grt *Ulysses* (Albert Wilhelmi Collection).

Right: Passenger ships of Germany's Woermann Line, which sailed to Africa, but as seen in Hamburg harbour (Richard Faber Collection).

Spanish flag service to North and West Africa on *Compania Trasmediterranea* (Author's Collection).

Off to the East Indies: a superb poster promoting Holland's Rotterdam Lloyd (Richard Faber Collection).

To Africa on the combination passenger-cargo ships of the Ellerman and Bucknall Lines (Author's Collection).

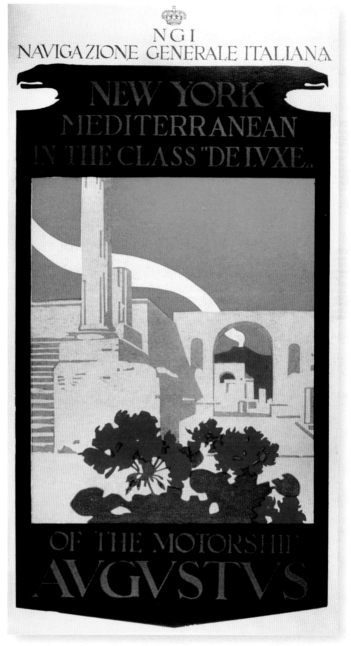

The biggest Italian liner yet, the 32,600grt *Augustus* (Richard Faber Collection).

An artist's rendering of Lloyd Sabaudo's Four Counts – *Conte Rosso, Conte Verde, Conte Biancamano* and *Conte Grande* (Richard Faber Collection).

The first-class dining room aboard the *Vulcania* of 1928 (Norman Knebel Collection).

The social hall on board the *Saturnia* (Norman Knebel Collection).

The *Saturnia* as seen in the 1950s
(James Sesta Collection).

The *Colombo* of Italy's Navigazione
Generale Italiana was primarily
a migrant ship (Richard Faber
Collection).

The *Vulcania* seen at sea (Richard Faber Collection).

SISTER MOTOR VESSELS

SATURNIA - VULCANIA

(24.000 GROSS TONS)
Maiden Voyage of the M/S „VULCANIA"
from TRIESTE: 19th December 1928.

Italian might and power: a wonderful if exaggerated view of the near-sisters *Saturnia* and *Vulcania* (Richard Faber Collection).

Right: Spanning the globe on Canadian Pacific (Author's Collection).

CANADIAN PACIFIC
SPANS THE WORLD

MOST CONVENIENT ROUTE TO
CANADA — U.S.A. — JAPAN — CHINA, NEW ZEALAND & AUSTRALIA.

Above: A superb depiction of the three-funnel *Empress of Canada*, used in transpacific service (Richard Faber Collection).

Left: A souvenir badge from the *Empress of Asia* (Richard Faber Collection).

Right: Hamburg South America Line to the ports along the east coast of South America (Richard Faber Collection).

HAMBURG SÜD-
AMERIKANISCHE DAMPF=
SCHIFFFAHRTS·GESELLSCHAFT

Hamburg, Holzbrücke 8.

Brasilien

Rio de Janeiro
São Francisco

Rio Grande
Buenos Aires

Argentinien

VON HAMBURG u. EMDEN
NACH BRASILIEN u. ARGENTINIEN

D. CAP POLONIO   D. ESPAÑA
D. ANTONIO DELFINO   D. LA CORUÑA
D. CAP NORTE   D. VIGO
D. ARGENTINA   D. TUCUMAN

Reisebureau Brasch & Rothenstein, Münche
Hotel Deutscher Kaiser, gegenüber dem Hauptbahnhof, Nordausgang

An artist's touch: the mighty *Cap Polonio* in Hamburg harbour (Hamburg South America Line).

The *Monte Sarmiento* in the foreground with the *Cap Polonio* behind (Hamburg South America Line).

Royal Mail's new *Alcantara* and *Asturias* were the new sensations on the UK–South America run in the late twenties (Author's Collection).

Hamburg America Line ran services from Northern Europe to the Caribbean, Central America and the West Coast of South America (Author's Collection).

NACH SÜDAMERIKA

LOHMANN

Überfahrtsbedingungen
für die dritte Klasse
HAMBURG-SÜDAMERIKANISCHE
DAMPFSCHIFFFAHRTS-GESELLSCHAFT

First class on board the great *Cap Arcona* of 1927 (Richard Faber Collection).

Hamburg South America's *Monte* class ships were very popular (Richard Faber Collection).

'The sun never sets on the NYK Line' noted this fine view of the *Chicibu Maru* departing (Richard Faber Collection).

A splendid depiction of the *Asama Maru* of NYK Line by Japanese artist Hayao Nogami (Hayao Nogami Collection).

Above: Another fine painting by Hayao Nogami, but of the *Chicibu Maru* (Hayao Nogami Collection).

Left: Sailing to South America on the Lamport & Holt Lines (Author's Collection).

Above: Cruising on Swedish America Line's *Gripsholm* (Richard Faber Collection).

Holiday cruising on White Star (Norman Knebel Collection).

Size comparison: the mighty *Bremen* passing a smaller North German Lloyd passenger ship (Hapag-Lloyd).

The *Columbus* was fitted with shorter, flatter funnels to better match the new *Europa* and *Bremen* (Hapag-Lloyd).

A poetic late day scene of the *Bremen,* the largest and mightiest liner built in the 1920s (Hapag-Lloyd).

Left: Ornate splendour! The main lounge aboard the 1,675-passenger *Roma* (Maurizio Eliseo Collection).

Right: Outbound from Genoa in 1936, the 709ft-long *Roma* has been repainted in all white for more extensive cruising (Paolo Piccione Collection).

Right: Classic motor ship design: the *Vulcania* has the long, low, rather flat look of motor liners of the 1920s. She is seen here passing Lower Manhattan in a view dated 1932 (Author's Collection).

Below: Post-war service: the *Vulcania* (left) and *Saturnia* are seen together in this view at Genoa from 1949 (Richard Faber Collection).

7

THE NEW MODERNE AND THE EXTRAORDINARY
ÎLE DE FRANCE

The French Government, as well as the French Line, the Compagnie Générale Transatlantique, were anxious to establish a strong and firm presence on the competitive North Atlantic run to New York. Beginning in 1909, they planned at least four successively larger luxury liners. The process began with the first French superliner, the 23,500grt, four-funnel *France* of 1912. The second ship, the *Paris*, was bigger still and due in 1916. The war changed that, of course. She was quietly launched at St Nazaire in 1916 but then put aside. When she finally emerged in the summer of 1921, the French could not have been more pleased. With her high speed and her stunning decor, she was an instant favourite. Decoratively, she was 'in a class by herself' according to liner historian Everett Viez. Few ships proved to be a better investment – the opulent first-class quarters on board the 34,569grt *Paris* had the lowest percentage of vacancies of all Atlantic liners in the twenties.

On board the 1,930-passenger *Paris*, the rich, gilded Louis XIV of earlier French liners gave way to a more startling Art Nouveau, even an early Art Deco. Notations included the salon de thé, where moderne was the style and all supplemented by light-coloured walls, indirect lighting and a large skylight. In the centre of the room was an illuminated dance floor. The first-class dining room had two levels. Her first-class suites were dubbed 'apartments at sea'. Then, of course, there was the magnificent French service and fine cuisine. 'It is harder to diet on the *Paris* than other liners,' wrote a New York reporter who crossed on board on a seven-night passage to Le Havre.

The *Paris* also had a sense of the dramatic. She rammed and sank a freighter in New York Harbor in October 1927, went aground at New York and then off the English coast in April 1929 and then had a near-fatal fire at her Le Havre berth in August 1929. She needed five months' repairs afterwards. Fire would spell, just as for many other French passenger ships, her end. She burned out at her Le Havre pier on 19 April 1939, capsized and became a complete loss. Her final remains were not removed until well after the war, in 1947.

One of the grandest and most popular Atlantic liners of the 1920s, the French Line's splendid *Paris* sails past Lower Manhattan in this 1930 view. She was off on another crossing, to Plymouth and Le Havre (Cronican-Arroyo Collection).

Innovative liner! The decoratively innovative and stunning *Île de France* sets off on her maiden voyage from Le Havre to New York in 1927 (French Line).

Maiden arrival at New York: the 791ft-long *Île de France* arrives at New York for the very first time and is about to be berthed at Pier 57 at the foot of West 15th Street (Richard Faber Collection).

years, she handled the luxury run to New York. She later became Canadian Pacific's *Empress of Australia* and then the Italian *Venezuela* before being scrapped in 1962.

One of the first, new, large liners to be designed and constructed after the First World War was the 43,153grt *Île de France*, completed in 1927. She was a follow-up to the earlier *France* and *Paris*, but with a significant difference: her decor was new and different, modernist and based on the 1925 Exposition of Art and Decoration in Paris. It was, in fact, the beginning of Art Deco on the high seas, 'ocean liner style' as it was also dubbed. It ignored the dark woods and heavy gilding of the past, but used lighter woods and colours, sleek and angular designs, and added touches such as tubular chairs and soft, indirect lighting. Other liners quickly followed the immensely popular *Île de France*, and later so did hotels, department stores, skyscrapers, railway terminals and Hollywood set designers. She was later called the 'floating Ginger Rogers'.

The *Île* had it all, so it seemed – the longest bar then afloat, a Parisian sidewalk café and even a real carousel (with painted ponies) in the children's playroom. Each of her 439 first-class staterooms was done in a different decor and, carrying more first-class passengers than any other Atlantic liner by the early thirties, the French Line noted there were also 'four apartments of great luxury and ten of luxury'. The first-class dining room, three decks in height, was one of 'massive simplicity' and likened to being like a 'modern

Chic style! The first-class main lounge aboard the 1,786-passenger *Île de France* (Andy Hernandez Collection)

Like many others, the French – including the French Line – built many intermediate, smaller passenger ships such as the 17,707grt, 2,111-passenger *De Grasse*, completed in 1924. She alternated: Le Havre–New York crossings, service from Le Havre to the Caribbean and also on periodic cruises. Sunk by the Nazis in 1944, she was salvaged, rebuilt and then this 574-footer became France's first, post-Second World War liner. For two

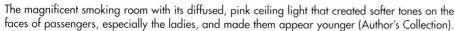

The magnificent smoking room with its diffused, pink ceiling light that created softer tones on the faces of passengers, especially the ladies, and made them appear younger (Author's Collection).

The first-class main foyer and staircase aboard the 23-knot, quadruple-screw Ile de France (Andy Hernandez Collection).

Greek temple'. The cuisine was, of course, exceptional and unsurpassable. It was quite true: 'More sea gulls followed the French liners than any other ships!'

The Île de France was in British hands during the war and served heroically as an Allied trooper. After extensive restoration and rebuilding in the late forties, she re-entered luxury service in the summer of 1949 with more modern interiors and the original three funnels replaced by two. She carried on until late 1958 and, while there were thoughts of preservation, she was sold to Japanese scrappers at Osaka. Sailing out to the East as the *Furansu Maru*, she had one last assignment: portraying the fictional liner *Claridon* in a Hollywood film, *The Last Voyage*. Partially sunk in the film's sequences, she was later brought into Osaka and demolished, ending an otherwise glorious career of thirty-two years.

8

CROSSING THE PACIFIC

Some travel pundits said that the very finest liner service on the Pacific was maintained by Canadian Pacific, the passenger ship arm of the great Anglo-Canadian travel empire (the company also had trains, hotels, small steamers and freighters and a separate Atlantic liner fleet). Instead of the Suez Canal, Canadian Pacific offered an alternate route to the Orient – crossing the Atlantic from Britain by liner, then across Canada by rail and finally across the Pacific by other company passenger liners. From Vancouver and nearby Victoria, it was five days to Honolulu, nine days to Yokohama, ten to Kobe, twelve to Shanghai, fifteen to Hong Kong and seventeen to Manila. First-class fares in 1929 were posted as $120 to Honolulu, $310 to Japan and $350 to China. European servants could accompany passengers for an entire one-way voyage for $110; Asian servants were charged $50. On the lower decks, there were dormitory quarters in third class – with fares from Shanghai to Vancouver of $115 with European food and $85 with Oriental food.

The four noted Canadian Pacific liners of the twenties were all three-stackers: the superb collection of *Empress of Asia*, *Empress of Canada*, *Empress of Russia* and *Empress of Australia*. The latter, a 21,860-tonner, was perhaps the most noted and famous. She had been a ship of reparations, coming to the company after the First World War. She was partially built as the *Tirpitz* for Hamburg America Line in 1913–14, but never completed owing to the outbreak of war. She sat incomplete throughout until 1919, when she ceded to Britain and then to Canadian Pacific. She became the *Empress of Australia* a year later, with accommodations for 1,513 passengers – 404 in first class, 165 second class, 270 third class and 674 steerage. Generally known as the 'Pacific Empresses', the *Empress of Australia* was also a heroic ship. She rescued over 2,000 people from the great Tokyo earthquake, which occurred on 1 September 1923. In addition to offering long, luxury cruises, the 615ft-long *Empress of Australia* carried Britain's King George VI and Queen Elizabeth on their North American tour, to Canada, in May 1939.

Increasingly, in the 1930s, Canadian Pacific faced greater competition on the transpacific run from the likes of America's Dollar Line and Japan's

NYK Line. They were prompted to strengthen their own operation with the 26,000grt *Empress of Japan*, added in 1930 and the fastest liner on the Pacific.

All ships were called to military duties in the autumn of 1939 and subsequently three became casualties. The *Empress of Russia* almost survived, but then was destroyed in a fire at a British shipyard in September 1945. On 5 February 1942, the *Empress of Asia* was attacked in Pacific waters by no less than twenty-seven Japanese bombers. With 2,651 on board, it was miraculous

The *Empress of Australia*, a great favourite on the Pacific, is seen here at Southampton on 25 May 1939. She had just returned from a crossing to Canada on which she carried King George VI and Queen Elizabeth on a goodwill tour of Canada and the United States (Cronican-Arroyo Collection).

Left: The first-class dining saloon with buffet aboard the 21,860-ton *Empress of Australia.* There was a musicians' gallery at the far end and over 150 items on the dinner menus (Cronican-Arroyo Collection).

Right: Pacific luxuries! The music room aboard the *Empress of Russia* (Cronican-Arroyo Collection).

Below: Inbound: The beautiful-looking *Empress of Russia* arriving at Vancouver (Albert Wilhelmi Collection).

that all but nineteen survived. Lastly, the *Empress of Canada* was torpedoed by an Italian submarine in the South Atlantic in 1943. Some 392 perished.

In 1945–46, Canadian Pacific thought briefly of restoring its Pacific service but then considered the much changed economic situation in Japan and the unstable political tone in China. The idea was abandoned. The surviving *Empress of Australia* became a migrant ship while the *Empress of Japan*, renamed *Empress of Scotland* in 1942, was restored for duties as the Line's transatlantic flagship.

Japan emerged with three significant transpacific liners, each constructed in the late 1920s. In a 1999 edition, a glossy Japanese shipping magazine ran a special feature – a tribute to a great national passenger ship. This was followed by a commemorative book, complete with vintage photos and architectural drawings. The huge NYK Line, Nippon Yusen Kaisha of Tokyo and today one of the world's largest shipowners and operators, took part. The subject was, after all, one of their most famous ships – the 16,975grt liner *Asama Maru*. It was the sixtieth anniversary of her commissioning, in October 1929. At 583ft in length, she was Japan's finest ocean liner yet and certainly their largest in the prestige service between the United States and the Orient. She remains also a 'grandmother' of sorts to the present, luxurious era of the *Crystal Symphony* and *Crystal Serenity*, operated by Los Angeles-based Crystal Cruises, a subsidiary of NYK, and to the *Asuka II*, the former *Crystal Harmony*, operated by NYK Cruises.

Built by Mitsubishi Shipbuilding & Engineering Company at their Nagasaki plant, the *Asama Maru* was fitted with Swiss-made Sulzer diesels and Western decor in her public areas. There was a smoking room done in Tudor, the first-class restaurant had a two-deck-high well and the first-class cabin accommodation included lavish suites complete with sitting areas. The ship's quarters were divided between 222 in first class, a small second

Japan's NYK Line offered special, reduced summer fares on its transpacific crossings. The Depression had taken its hold and some passenger loads had lessened. The advert dates from February 1932 (*National Geographic* magazine).

The short-lived American Oriental Mail Line offered service every twelve days from Seattle via Victoria to Yokohama, Kobe, Shanghai, Hong Kong and Manila (National Geographic Society).

class for 96 and then an austere third class with 504 berths, many of them in dormitories for immigrants. The *Asama Maru*, which entered Pacific service at the time of the infamous Wall Street Crash, in October 1929, was followed by a twin sister, the *Tatsuta Maru* (a name amended to *Tatuta Maru* in 1938) and which was commissioned in April 1930. A third, slightly larger ship, the *Chichibu Maru* (which was renamed *Kamakura Maru* in 1939), was added to NYK service, quite uniquely, in the very same month. The latter ship was also noticeably different in having one squat funnel whereas the earlier pair had twin stacks.

The *Asama Maru*, which was dubbed 'Queen of the Pacific', and her two fleetmates were routed from Los Angeles and San Francisco to Honolulu, Yokohama, Kobe, Shanghai and Manila. San Francisco to Honolulu took five days where it was fifteen days to Yokohama (for Tokyo) and twenty days to Shanghai. First-class fares started at $315 for the San Francisco–Yokohama voyage and from $361 for the journey to Shanghai. 'Before the Second World War, Japanese vessels were the favourite Pacific ships to many tourists,' wrote the late ocean liner historian and author Frank Braynard:

Tea ceremonies, Japanese wrestling bouts, quaintly bowing officers and other attractions added to the Oriental atmosphere. Even the American and Canadian Pacific ships on these same routes adopted Eastern styles in decoration and cuisine. NYK was especially noted for its fine food. A typical menu offered a curious mixture of Russian, Chinese, American, Japanese, English, Greek, Dutch and French dishes.

The pride of the entire Japanese fleet, the 19-knot *Asama Maru*, was nearly lost in September 1937. While undergoing repairs at the Taikoo Dockyard at Hong Kong, typhoon warnings prompted a move of the ship to a safe anchorage in Sai Wan Bay. The force of the hurricane was so great, however, that the ship's starboard anchor and then port anchor snapped and the liner was tossed ashore in an almost ballasted condition. At first, it appeared that the vessel was lost, but the Tokyo-based Nippon Salvage Company was hired and given the difficult task of refloating the badly stranded ship on a 'no cure – no pay' basis. In order to get the *Asama Maru* off at high tide, some 3,500 tons of material, including two of the four main engines, had to be removed and placed in barges. In addition, 7,500 tons of rock was dredged away from the hull using 2½ tons of explosives. Six months later, in March 1938, she was finally refloated. The strenuous efforts included 41,196 man days of labour of which 5,586 were diver days. She returned to Japan for repairs, which took another six months. In all, the *Asama Maru* was out of commercial service for a year.

ROOM AND BATH
ROUND THE WORLD

$1370.

A palatial Liner becomes your home for 20,236 miles.

You have a large outside room with twin beds, and your private bath. Delicious meals, interesting friends. Your living room window will look out upon the great ports of the world, which you will visit...Yokohama...Kobe...Shanghai...Hong Kong...Manila...Singapore, etc...And this acme of travel experience, a trip Round the World, is now yours *in luxury* at the rate of $16.11 per day. Room, bath, meals—and Round the World!

You are free to stop over where you like, as long as you like. Your ticket is good for two years. Visit any land that interests you, continue your journey on another President Liner as you would on another train. No other plan of world travel offers

Outdoor swimming pool on board

you such freedom, such comfort, such consideration for your personal wishes.

This is your world—give yourself the experience of a lifetime and see it! Visit lands you have read about, heard others discuss, and longed to see in the real. And go, not as a scheduled tourist, but as a traveler—with home always in the harbor when you want it!

INFORMATION SAILINGS

Every week a palatial President Liner sails from Los Angeles and San Francisco—via the Sunshine Belt—for Honolulu, Japan, China, Manila and thence every two weeks to Malaya—Java nearby—Ceylon, (India by Pullman overnight), Egypt, Italy, France, New York.

Fortnightly sailings from Boston, New York via Havana, Panama to California, and Round the World.

Fortnightly sailings from Seattle and Victoria, B. C., for Japan, China, Manila and Round the World.

($1370 up—fare provides First Class accommodations in twin bed stateroom, bath and meals, also rail fare from any direct line point in the U.S. to Los Angeles, San Francisco, Seattle or Victoria, B. C., and back to starting point from New York.)

Ask for further information from any steamship or tourist agent.

COMPLETE INFORMATION FROM ANY STEAMSHIP OR TOURIST AGENT

AMERICAN MAIL LINE AND DOLLAR STEAMSHIP LINES

604 FIFTH AVE., NEW YORK . . . . . N. Y.	201 BROADWAY	406 THIRTEENTH ST. . . . . OAKLAND, CALIF.
25 AND 32 BROADWAY . . . . NEW YORK	210 SO. SIXTEENTH ST. . . . SAN DIEGO, CALIF.	909 GOVERNMENT ST., . . . VICTORIA, B. C.
110 SOUTH DEARBORN ST. . . . CHICAGO	DIME BANK BLDG. . . . . PHILADELPHIA	517 GRANVILLE ST., . . . VANCOUVER, B. C.
UNION TRUST ARCADE . . . CLEVELAND	1005 CONNECTICUT N. W., . . DETROIT	32 VIA VITTORIO VENETO . . . ROME, ITALY
177 STATE ST. . . . . BOSTON, MASS.	152 BROADWAY . . . WASH., D. C.	11 BIS RUE SCRIBE . . . . PARIS, FRANCE
514 W. SIXTH ST. . . . LOS ANGELES, CALIF.	YOKOHAMA KOBE PORTLAND, OREGON	22 BILLITER ST. . . . . E. C. 3, LONDON
ROBERT DOLLAR BLDG. . . . SAN FRANCISCO	HONG KONG MANILA SHANGHAI	4TH AT UNIVERSITY . . . SEATTLE, WASH.

Above: The American Mail Line and Dollar Steamship Line offered co-ordinated services which included transpacific service as well as 100-night voyages around the world. A highlighted selling point: 'Room, bath, meals – and around the world at a rate of $16.11 per day'. This promotion dates from February 1930 (*National Geographic* magazine).

Right: The 17,491-ton *Aorangi*, built in 1924 for the Union Steamship Company of New Zealand (and later operated by the Canadian-Australian Line), offered regular sailings between Australia, New Zealand and Vancouver. She endured until scrapped in 1953 (Cronican-Arroyo Collection).

Sadly, almost all Japanese liners were lost in the Second World War. The *Asama Maru* was among them. She was used for a time as a troop transport and also as a diplomatic exchange ship. In the summer of 1942, she was sent to Lourenco Marques in Portuguese East Africa for a rendezvous with another exchange ship, Sweden's *Gripsholm*. Refugees and prisoners were swapped between the two former luxury liners. The *Asama Maru* became a casualty toward the end of the war. She was torpedoed and sunk by an American submarine while sailing in the China Sea. By the war's end, in August 1945, only the 11,000-ton *Hikawa Maru* survived in the once mighty NYK Line passenger fleet. Ships like the *Asama Maru* are still well remembered, however.

The Union Steamship Company of New Zealand, based in London, added the imposing 17,500grt *Aorangi* for their South Pacific service between Sydney, Auckland and Vancouver in 1924.

Japan's *Asama Maru* passes under the San Francisco–Oakland Bay Bridge in this view from 1938 (Author's Collection).

9

THE *CAP ARCONA* AND THE SOUTHERN SEAS

In the twenties, the liner run between Europe and the East Coast of South America was busy. There was a trade of businessmen, some tourists and a large flow of westbound migrants, especially from Portugal and Spain. Several companies capitalised on this, one being Germany's Hamburg South America Line. They created a considerable fleet of liners especially for this run. The largest after the First World War was the 20,576grt *Cap Polonio*, which was under construction in the dramatic peace-breaking summer of 1914. The 662-footer was being built at the famed Blohm & Voss shipyard at Hamburg. The 17-knot ship was later completed as an armed merchant cruiser for the Kaiser's navy and named *Vineta*. It was all quite unsuccessful and the ship reverted to being the intended *Cap Polonio*. She was ceded to the British in 1919, just after the war ended, and did temporary service for both the Union-Castle and P&O lines, under her German name as well, but was not retained. She was returned to the Germans, to Hamburg South America, in 1921 and refitted to her luxurious Teutonic standard. She became the finest liner based in northern Europe on the South American run, running from Hamburg to Rio de Janeiro, Santos, Montevideo and Buenos Aires. She could carry 1,555 passengers – 356 in superb first class, 250 second class and 949 third class.

A splendid-looking ship with her trio of white funnels capped by red bands, she was a victim of the Depression. After only a decade of service, she was laid up in 1931, briefly served as a moored exhibition ship at Hamburg in 1933 and then, in 1935, was sold for scrapping.

The migrant trade from Portugal and Spain was immense, growing and hugely appealing to companies like Hamburg South America. It all prompted the German directors to construct no less than five twin-funnel sister ships – comfortable, sturdy but not overly luxurious ships. The 13,882-ton *Monte Sarmiento* was first, being commissioned in November 1924, and was followed by the *Monte Olivia* (1924), *Monte Cervantes* (1928), *Monte Pascoal* (1931) and finally the *Monte Rosa* (1932). On board the 524ft-long *Monte Rosa*, the accommodation suited the trade – 2,408 passengers divided between 1,372 tourist class and 1,036 steerage. For cruises, the steerage space was sealed off. The galleys on board were noted to prepare 2,500 meals three times a day.

The Monte ships were popular cruise ships. They cruised from Hamburg and other European ports to the Baltic, Norwegian fjords, the British Isles, Canary Islands, West Africa, Spain, Portugal and the Mediterranean. They were also frequently chartered by the Nazi regime for so-called *Kraft durch Freunde* ('Strength through Joy') cruises.

The *Monte Cervantes* ran aground and was wrecked on 25 July 1928 near Tierra del Fuego. The other sisters were war losses with the exception of the *Monte Rosa*, which went on to become the British peacetime trooper *Empire Windrush*. She caught fire in the western Mediterranean on 28 March 1954, was abandoned and then sank five days later.

Fleetmates! The *Cap Arcona* (left) and the earlier *Cap Polonio* at Hamburg in the 1930s (Richard Faber Collection).

Above: German splendour! The magnificent *Cap Arcona*, Germany's largest and finest liner on the South Atlantic run to South America, loads passengers at the overseas landing stage at Hamburg (Author's Collection).

Above: Underway! The 27,650grt *Cap Arcona* departs Hamburg and begins her voyage to Southern ports – to Rio de Janeiro, Santos, Montevideo and Buenos Aires (Author's Collection).

Below: The *Monte Cervantes* was one of a class of ships built by the Hamburg South America Line for low-fare and migrant services to and from South America. These ships were also used for bargain cruises (Richard Faber Collection).

Left: German style! The grand smoking room aboard the 1,315-passenger *Cap Arcona* (Richard Faber Collection).

Far left: The smoking room aboard the *Monte Rosa* (Richard Faber Collection).

Left: Royal Mail Lines' *Alcantara* berthed at Southampton (Michael Cassar Collection).

Below: The first-class dining room aboard the 1,430-passenger *Alcantara*, a liner completed in 1927 (Richard Faber Collection).

Unquestionably, the largest, finest and grandest of the Hamburg South America liners was the 27,650grt *Cap Arcona*. Built at Hamburg, she was commissioned in November 1927. Said to be the finest way to sail between Europe and South America, her first class appealed to rich businessmen as well as European and Latin American aristocrats. There was a fine winter garden (complete with greenery and rattan chairs), a main hall (which resembled the finest hotels in Berlin and Buenos Aires) and a tile-faced indoor pool.

Quite sadly, the beautiful, very popular, 676ft-long *Cap Arcona* had a most tragic ending. Taken over by the German Navy in 1940, she was moored in occupied Gdynia in Poland for the next four years as an accommodation ship. She was reactivated in the winter of 1945 for the huge effort of evacuating the Eastern Territories, which were in fast retreat. Alone, the *Cap Arcona* transported 26,000 people in three voyages home to Germany. The fourth trip, in April, was her last as she embarked 5,000 prisoners from the Neuengamme concentration camp plus 1,000 others including crew. On 3 May, the former queen of the South Atlantic was attacked by British fighter-bombers and caught fire. All means of rescue were impossible. Meanwhile, panic broke out on board and, shortly afterwards, the liner capsized. Although the ship was lying only a few hundred yards from shore, with a third of her width out of the water, the disaster claimed some 5,000 lives. The death of these concentration camp prisoners was all the more tragic since they would have been liberated in a matter of days. The wreckage of the *Cap Arcona* was broken up in the late 1940s.

British flag service to South America was dominated by the London-based Royal Mail Lines. Their position was greatly strengthened in the mid-twenties when they ordered a pair of 22,000-ton motor liners, the sister ships

Asturias and *Alcantara*. They had splendid passenger quarters, especially in first class, provision for immigrants in third class, and especially large cargo capacities, which added to their blend of revenues. Along with the mail, these 656ft-long sisters carried general British-manufactured goods on the southbound trips and then returned with the likes of Argentine beef and Brazilian coffee. Carrying 1,410 passengers (410 first class, 232 second class, 768 third class) on the *Asturias*, the two liners were routed from Southampton and Cherbourg via Corunna and Vigo in Spain and Lisbon in Portugal to Pernambuco, Bahia, Rio de Janeiro, Santos, Montevideo and Buenos Aires. The voyage from Southampton to Buenos Aires took just short of three weeks. A roundtrip first-class ticket was priced at $375.

The passenger-cargo liner *Highland Princess*, also belonging to Britain's Royal Mail Lines, is outbound from London's Tilbury Docks on a voyage to ports along the East Coast of South America (Richard Faber Collection).

Blue Star Line was another entrant in the South American trade and used ships such as the 164-passenger *Arandora*. Built in 1927, she was rebuilt a year later as a cruise ship (for 354 passengers) and renamed *Arandora Star*. She was one of Britain's finest and most popular cruise ships of the 1930s (Alex Duncan).

Another British shipping firm, Furness Withy & Company, had an arm known as the Furness Prince Line, which, beginning in 1929, ran a quartet of 101-bed combo ships on the New York–South America run. Shown here, the 10,900grt *Eastern Prince* survived the Second World War, but was to spend her remaining days as the troopship *Empire Medway* (Alex Duncan).

Still another British shipping company, the Lamport & Holt Line ran ships such as their *Voltaire* on a similar service – from New York to South America's East Coast ports (Albert Wilhelmi Collection).

TRAVEL INTEREST TURNS TO SOUTH AMERICA

The "FOUR PRINCES"

"Northern Prince," "Eastern Prince," "Southern Prince," "Western Prince"—already these names are a byword in the trip between New York and Rio de Janeiro, Santos, Montevideo and Buenos Aires. Already the prospects of travel are brightened by their modern luxury, by their safety, by the speed and vibrationless power of their twin Diesel motors.

Accommodations for first-class passengers only. Reservations and literature at authorized tourist agents, or address Furness Prince Line, 34 Whitehall St. (where Broadway begins), or 565 Fifth Avenue, New York City.

Prince Line Service has been continuous between New York and South America for 35 years.

FURNESS-*Prince* LINE

An advertisement for the Furness Prince Line and its four combination passenger-cargo ships (*National Geographic* magazine).

First-class public rooms were fashioned after British and Empire domestic styles and included a two-deck main dining room (on board the *Asturias*) in French Empire style and large enough to seat 400 at one time. There were also Moorish tones in some public areas, a sumptuous winter garden and a prized amenity: a 29ft-long indoor swimming pool.

The twin liners gained lots of publicity because of their propulsion. Instead of the customary steam turbines, they were given the new, supposedly more efficient diesels. The Danish-made diesels gave, it was said, a smoother as well as more efficient ride. They also eliminated the need for a big boiler room. Significantly, the ships had a modern exterior – two squat funnels (the forward one was, in fact, a dummy). These diesels proved ineffective, however, by 1934 when the Royal Mail wanted a faster service speed for an accelerated service to South America. The pair were soon fitted with classic steam turbines, two larger funnels and their service speed increased by 2 knots, from 16 to 18 knots.

The *Asturias* was badly damaged in the Second World War, but later repaired for use as both a peacetime troopship and part-time migrant ship until scrapped in 1957; the *Alcantara* survived the war intact and returned to the South American liner run until demolished in 1958.

Augmenting the British presence on the South American run was the Nelson Line, which added no less than six motor liners, beginning in 1928. They too were motor ships and with squat funnels, but also had broken superstructures with bridge and officer quarters separated by a cargo hold and then the passenger accommodations. At just over 14,000 tons, they were named *Highland Monarch*, *Highland Chieftain*, *Highland Brigade*, *Highland Hope*, *Highland Princess* and, completed in 1932, *Highland Patriot*. Nelson fell on hard financial times, however, as the Depression tightened its grip and so, by 1932, was absorbed by the larger, financially stronger Royal Mail Lines. Several of these Highland ships would serve Royal Mail until as late as 1960.

Britain's Pacific Steam Navigation Company created five sisters – the 15,600grt *Orbita* and her sisters *Orduna*, *Orca*, *Oropesa* and *Oroya* – just after the war. Mostly, these ships sailed to South American ports, but went to West Coast ports as far south as Valparaiso on voyages from Liverpool.

While mostly interested in the northbound Argentine meat trade, another British firm, the Blue Star Line, built five new combination all-first-class passenger ships for the run between London and the east coast of South America. The series began in 1926 with the 12,800grt, 180-passenger *Almeda* (soon changed to *Almeda Star*), *Andalucia* (*Andalucia Star*), *Avila* (*Avila Star*),

Far left: An American firm, the Munson Line, ran four ships as well – the *American Legion, Pan America, Western World* and *Southern Cross* – with sailings every other week from New York to South America (*National Geographic* magazine).

Left: The Great White Fleet, as it was called, of the New York-based United Fruit Company ran eleven- to twenty-four-day voyages to the Caribbean and Central America (*National Geographic* magazine).

Avelona (*Avelona Star*) and finally *Arandora* (*Arandora Star*). The *Avelona Star* was later withdrawn from passenger service and rebuilt as a freighter; meanwhile, the *Arandora Star* underwent a series of enhancing refits that made the 354-passenger ship into one of Britain's finest and most popular cruise ships.

Away from home waters, another British company, the Furness Prince Line, created a quartet of handsome passenger–cargo ships, the 10,900grt, 100-passenger *Northern Prince, Eastern Prince, Southern Prince* and *Western Prince*. They were used in the New York–East Coast of South America service. Still another firm, the Lamport & Holt Line, also involved in the New York–South America trade, added the 13,200grt sisters *Vandyck* and *Voltaire*.

To strengthen their competition with the nearby Italians out of the Mediterranean, France's Transports Maritimes added several new ships including the 10,800grt, 1,308-passenger *Campana*. A twin-funnel liner that sailed until the 1970s (but in later years as Italy's *Irpinia*), she sailed between Marseilles and the east coast of South America.

10

THE *STELLA POLARIS* AND CRUISING TO THE SUN

While luxury cruising began almost a century earlier, it was a very specialised, sporadic business. The 1920s saw a new growth and greater popularity, however. As shipowners noted considerable drops in transatlantic passenger loads in the depths of winter, they sent such celebrated, big liners such as the *Mauretania*, *Aquitania* and *Homeric* off on long, luxurious trips of one and two months in length to the Caribbean, South America and the Mediterranean. American millionaires in particular loved them – long wintertime sojourns away from the cold weather. Along with steamer trunks, many brought their personal servants along.

Luxury cruising took a great jump in 1927. When built by Sweden's Götaverken Shipyard that year, the *Stella Polaris* was the finest passenger ship designed exclusively for cruising. She was built for Norway's Bergen Line, which had offered summertime leisure voyages along the Norwegian coast,

but now wanted to expand to worldwide cruise itineraries. The new ship was a major investment, costing 4 million Swedish Kronor.

She was built to resemble a luxury yacht, in fact a lavish royal yacht. She had two tall masts, a bowsprit and a counter stern, all of which made her a most attractive vessel. Almost immediately, she was a favourite of the wealthy. Accommodation was in especially spacious cabins, many of them with private bathroom facilities, and was limited to 190 passengers maximum. Between 1927 and the outbreak of war in the autumn of 1939, this elegant ship was seen in northern Europe, the Mediterranean, the Caribbean and in the South Sea islands of the Pacific. In the 1930s, she made a number of four-month-long around-the-world cruises. 'She was a ship of quiet luxury – polished woods, smorgasbord lunches, afternoon teas and fine Scandinavian service,' according to Everett Viez.

When war began and Norway was occupied, the *Stella Polaris* was laid up in the Osterfjord, just north of Bergen. Here, the Nazis used her, from 1943, as an accommodation ship for U-boat crews based at Narvik. She survived, quite fortunately, and had a brief stint as a troopship in 1945. Over the winter of 1945–46, the 416ft-long *Stella Polaris* was completely refitted and restored by her Swedish builders.

In the autumn of 1946, the *Stella Polaris* resumed full-time cruising – sailing to New Orleans for a series of voyages to the Caribbean. In 1951, she did another world cruise, but was soon sold, going to the Swedish flag for the Malmo-based Clipper Line. Clipper operated her, as the 'Queen of the Oceans', on basically Europe in summer and the Caribbean in winter

In this view, dated 16 September 1955, the striking *Stella Polaris* is berthed behind the Italian *Argentina* at Valletta in Malta. The *Stella*, it was reported, had arrived with 150 American and European tourists onboard a long cruise that began in Copenhagen and included stops at the likes of Dover, Boulogne, Lisbon and Tangiers. Afterward, the itinerary included the Greek isles, Sicily, Monte Carlo and then to Southampton and ending at Copenhagen (Cronican-Arroyo Collection).

The handsome, if ill-fated, *Bermuda* approaching Pier 95 at New York (Author's Collection).

schedules, until 1969. At that time, aged 42, she was sold to Japanese buyers, who moored the ship in Mitohama Bay, north of Tokyo, for use as a hotel and entertainment ship. She was renamed *Scandinavia*. In later years, she was renamed as *Stella Polaris*. In 2006, she was to be returned to Europe for use as a hotel in Stockholm harbour. Leaving her berth for the first time in some thirty-five years, she was unsuited for deep-sea sailing and sank, on 2 September, in waters off southern Japan.

During the twenties, long, luxury cruises greatly increased – no doubt in part for the escapism they provided. Millionaires, usually Americans, liked staying aboard ships for months at a time. Red Star Line's 24,578grt *Belgenland* was often chartered out for around-the-world cruises, voyages of up to 150 days touching on as many as sixty ports in fourteen countries and covering over 28,000 miles. Cruising spread to Europe as well. In Britain, the combination passenger-cargo ship *Arandora*, carrying 164 all-first-class passengers, was refitted in 1928–29 as the *Arandora Star*. Now that she was a full-time cruising ship her capacity increased to 354 vacationers.

Short cruising was on the rise as well. Britain's large Furness Withy shipping group had many offshoots, one of which was the Furness Bermuda Line. They had great success in an infant holiday run between New York and Bermuda. Realising the potential, they added the 19,086grt *Bermuda* in 1927.

A fine-looking ship, she was much like an Atlantic liner and had superior accommodation for 700, mostly first-class passengers. Unfortunately, she was a most unlucky ship. She was badly damaged by fire at Bermuda in June 1931. Then she burned out completely while undergoing repairs at Belfast that November. She sank, but the wreckage was raised and sold for scrap. Finally, she ran aground while en route to Scotland for scrapping in June 1932. Her final remains were eventually demolished.

The American cruise industry expanded with more new ships for leisure voyages. Matson Line, based in San Francisco, saw great potential in the Hawaiian trade. So, for the San Francisco–Los Angeles–Honolulu run, the company added the 17,232grt *Malolo* in 1927. She was the first true luxury liner for Hawaiian service. Carrying just under 700 passengers, mostly in high-standard, first-class accommodation, she was a most advanced ship, especially for safety. Her design included advanced compartmentation systems. On her trials in the western Atlantic, the 582ft-long ship had a collision with a freighter that had an impact equal to that which sent the far larger *Titanic* to the bottom fifteen years earlier. The 21-knot *Malolo* survived and continued onward to New York flooded with 5,000 tons of sea water.

For its South American services, the New York-based Grace Line introduced the 8,000grt, 157-passenger sisters *Santa Maria* and *Santa Barbara*. US-flag ships, they were unique in being built in Britain and being diesel driven. A third sister, the *Santa Clara*, was constructed closer to home, in New Jersey. Another New York-based shipowner, the Panama Pacific Line,

After two devastating fires, the 4-year-old luxury cruise ship *Bermuda* is about to be scrapped. Her wrecked remains are seen here at Belfast (Richard K. Morse Collection).

Outbound for California via the Panama Canal, Panama Pacific Line's 20,300-ton *California* was one of three near-sisters used in that service. The *California* carried 747 passengers – 384 first class and 363 tourist class (Gillespie-Faber Collection).

Mini-liners: the 6,200-ton sisters *Iroquois* (shown here while aground along the Maine coast) and *Shawnee* resembled Atlantic liners, if small ones, with their twin funnels. They ran coastal services such as New York to Miami as well as cruises to the likes of Bermuda, Nassau, the Caribbean and, in summertime, to eastern Canada (Author's Collection).

In the late 1930s, these Panama Pacific liners were rebuilt for New York–South America sailings, often also offered as thirty-eight-day cruises. The former *Virginia* became the *Brazil*, sailing for Moore-McCormack Lines. She is seen here during a special call at Hamilton, Bermuda (Richard Faber Collection).

Right: Banana boats such as the 165-passenger *Toloa* of the United Fruit Company were popular for two- to three-week voyages to the Caribbean islands as well as more remote ports in Central America. The *Toloa* is seen here loading at Pier 3 in Lower Manhattan (Richard Faber Collection).

created a trio of 20,000-tonners in 1928–29. Named *California*, *Pennsylvania* and *Uruguay*, they were used in intercoastal service – between New York, Los Angeles and San Francisco via the Caribbean and Panama Canal.

Cruises of fourteen to twenty-one nights were also offered on the white-hulled ships of the United Fruit Company. So-called 'banana boats', they sailed to tropic ports in the Caribbean and Central America and offered leisurely, unpretentious, undemanding voyages. They were especially popular with retirees and with school teachers on summer holidays.

Other American shipowners such as the Clyde Mallory Lines added to its fine fleet of 'mini liners' – smallish passenger ships for the US coastal trades and cruising. Passengers could board in New York and do a cruise to Miami and back for $45. Two of the largest and finest ships for these short-sea services were the 754-bed sisters *Iroquois* and *Shawnee*. With twin funnels, they were indeed mini liners. Clyde Mallory had many other, but smaller, passenger ships – such as the 5,900grt *Cherokee*, *Seminole*, *Mohawk* and *Algonquin*, built in 1924. Another firm, the Eastern Steamship Lines, added four new steamers – the *Evangeline*, *Yarmouth*, *Acadia* and *St John* – for their services to New England and Canada. A mini voyage, say overnight from New York to Boston, could cost as little as $6 in a shared cabin.

Above: The United American Lines offered a fine roster of cruises – from 14 days to the Caribbean to 125 days around the world (National Geographic Society).

Left: Cruises became increasingly popular during the 1920s, but even in the lean Depression-era thirties. Munson Line offered the likes of twenty-five days for $200 or $8 per person per day (National Geographic Society).

Left: Panama Pacific Line's services included one way by liner between New York and California and the alternate by rail (National Geographic Society).

Above: When introduced in 1927, the *Malolo*, carrying 693 all-first-class passengers only, brought new levels of luxury to the California–Hawaii trade. Singlehandedly, the 17,232grt ship revolutionised tourism to the Hawaiian islands (Matson Lines).

LONG WINTER CRUISES 1928–29

ROUND THE WORLD

Dec 1st	*Empress of Australia*	136 days	from $1,900
Dec 17th	*Belgenland*	135 days	from $1,750
Jan 7th	*Resolute*	140 days	from $2,000
Jan 15th	*Franconia*	136 days	from $2,000

SOUTH AMERICA & AROUND AFRICA

Jan 12th	*Carinthia*	80 days	from $1,250
Jan 22nd	*Duchess of Atholl*	104 days	from $1,500

MEDITERRANEAN & HOLY LAND

Dec 5th	*Samaria*	43 days	from $655
Jan 5th	*France*	30 days	from $600
Jan 3rd	*Augustus*	23 days	from $275
Jan 4th	*Conte Grande*	24 days	from $275
Jan 10th	*Adriatic*	45 days	from $695
Jan 19th	*Laurentic*	45 days	from $695
Jan 22nd	*Samaria*	66 days	from $1,000
Jan 26th	*Homeric*	67 days	from $1,000
Jan 26th	*Conte Biancamano*	24 days	from $275
Jan 29th	*Scythia*	60 days	from $950
Jan 30th	*Transylvania*	66 days	from $1,750
Jan 31st	*St Louis*	70 days	from $900
Feb 2nd	*Roma*	23 days	from $275
Feb 4th	*Empress of Scotland*	72 days	from $900
Feb 7th	*Rotterdam*	72 days	from $955
Feb 9th	*France*	30 days	from $600
Feb 14th	*Calgaric*	68 days	from $740
Feb 16th	*Mauretania*	40 days	from $840
Feb 28th	*Adriatic*	45 days	from $695
Mar 9th	*Laurentic*	45 days	from $695
Mar 16th	*France*	30 days	from $600
Apr 8th	*Carinthia*	42 days	from $750

LONG WEST INDIES CRUISES

Jan 10th	*Duchess of Bedford*	29 days	from $300
Jan 19th	*California*	31 days	from $300
Jan 24th	*Reliance*	27 days	from $300
Jan 30th	*Columbus*	25 days	from $400
Jan 31st	*Lapland*	22 days	from $250
Feb 11th	*Duchess of Bedford*	29 days	from $300
Feb 12th	*Veendam*	30 days	from $385
Feb 23rd	*California*	31 days	from $300
Feb 23rd	*Reliance*	27 days	from $300
Feb 26th	*Columbus*	25 days	from $400

11

GERMAN MIGHT: THE RECORD-BREAKING *EUROPA* AND *BREMEN*

It seemed a fitting end of a decade: the creation of the German superliners *Europa* and *Bremen*. They were among the biggest, fastest and finest liners yet built. They were also two of the most important liners of the twentieth century.

It was quite extraordinary how the Germans regained transatlantic supremacy by 1930. They had lost almost all of their ships just a dozen or so years before, in 1918–19, at the end of the First World War. Britain held the prestigious Blue Riband with Cunard's exceptional *Mauretania* as well as the title of 'world's largest ship' with White Star Line's 56,600grt *Majestic*. But by 1927–28, German shipyard crews at Hamburg and at *Bremen* were

busily building what would become the mightiest liners yet – the twin speed champions *Europa* and *Bremen*. Intended to be 35,000-tonners and very similar to the existing *Columbus*, North German Lloyd had a change in plans and had the two new ships redesigned at over 50,000 tons and with far more powerful steam turbines.

The pair were launched a day apart in August 1928 – the *Europa* at the big Blohm & Voss shipyard at Hamburg on the 15th, the *Bremen* at the A.G. Weser Shipyard in *Bremen* a day later. What triumph! What publicity! What anticipation! The public was fascinated not only by their size and

Far left: After nearly being totally destroyed in a fire at the shipbuilders' yard, the 49,746grt *Europa* was repaired and readied for service to New York, if a year or so late. The liner is seen here, in a view dated 5 March 1930, being escorted by tugs in Hamburg harbour following successful sea trials (Cronican-Arroyo Collection).

Left: A dramatic view of the bow of the 936ft-long *Europa* (Cronican-Arroyo Collection).

luxuries, but by their great power. The *Bremen* snatched the coveted Ribbon from the British on her maiden crossing in July 1929. Her average speed was 27.8 knots. The *Europa* was to have been completed at the same time, in fact with fanciful rumours of dual German maiden voyages and dual record speeds, but she caught fire at the shipyard when nearly complete, on 26 March 1929. Damages were extensive and expensive, and she might even have been scrapped, but repairs were made and the 936ft-long liner had her debut in the following spring. The *Europa* then did even slightly better, at 27.9 knots. The Germans finally lost out to Italy's *Rex* three years later, in 1933. The two ships, assisted by the slightly smaller *Columbus*, ran a weekly service between Bremerhaven, Southampton, Cherbourg and New York. Accommodations on board the *Europa*, as an example, were divided between 687 in first class, 524 in second class, 306 tourist class and finally 507 third class. The 49,746grt liner was manned by a crew of 970.

'I saw the *Bremen* in the early thirties, docked at the Brooklyn Army Terminal, in New York's Lower Bay, because no large New York City pier was available to handle her or the *Europa*,' remembered the late Everett Viez, an ocean liner historian, photographer and New York City-based travel agent. 'She was immaculate. All spit 'n' polish. Her teak decks, for example, were snow white.'

'The *Bremen* and *Europa* were superb pieces of marine architecture,' added Viez:

> They were typically German modern with very contemporary, very nice interiors. But they suffered from anti-German feelings – left over from the First World War and then because of the rising Nazi movement. Passengers also often resented the aloof, sometimes cold attitude of their Teutonic crews. The important American Jewish trade soon avoided them altogether.

When film queen Marlene Dietrich was sailing to Europe on the *Bremen* in 1935, she found the ship to have 'Nazis everywhere'. There were banners and Swastikas, she reported, and copies of Hitler's Mein Kampf being sold in the shops. A fierce anti-Nazi, she firmly announced: 'This will be my last trip on a German ship!' She was soon travelling on liners such as the *Paris*, *Normandie*, *Berengaria* and *Queen Mary*.

After the *Normandie* and then the *Queen Mary* took the Atlantic record, beginning in 1935–36, there were rumours that Hitler wanted the *Europa* and *Bremen* to be re-engined so as to regain the Ribbon. In fact, this could not have happened without problems and strains on their hulls. North German Lloyd did, however, plan for the 'ultimate' German, and therefore

Left: Because of the unavailability of suitable piers in New York City, from 1929 until 1934, the *Bremen* (shown here) and *Europa* were forced to use a more distant facility – Pier 4 at the Army Terminal at the bottom end of the Brooklyn waterfront (Cronican-Arroyo Collection).

Below: Soon fitted with taller funnels for better smoke emission, the *Bremen* (left) and *Europa* are seen berthed together at the Columbus Quay at Bremerhaven (Hapag-Lloyd).

Nazi, transatlantic liner in the early 1940s. It was to be the 90,000grt *Amerika*, a projected ship later renamed *Viktoria*, but finally abandoned altogether as the Third Reich's wartime plans and advances reversed.

In the late 1930s, both the *Bremen* and *Europa* did some cruising as well – short trips to Bermuda and *Nassau*, the Caribbean and the occasional longer voyage. 'Both ships were actually too big at the time for cruising,' added Viez:

Left: Elegance at sea! Evening in the main lounge aboard the *Bremen* in the 1930s (Hapag-Lloyd).

Right: German decor! The first-class library aboard the 2,200-passenger *Bremen* (Hapag-Lloyd).

Below: The first-class ballroom aboard the 27-knot *Bremen* (Hapag-Lloyd).

The *Bremen*'s 1938 cruise around South America was actually a test by the Nazi Government to see if the ship could easily pass through the Panama Canal. She actually paid a record fee for the transit as well – $15,143.50 in all – and was the largest liner to pass through the canal until the 67,000grt *Queen Elizabeth 2* in 1975. She was chartered for this luxury voyage by Raymond Whitcomb, then a very large New York travel firm. But that voyage on board the *Bremen* almost ruined them! She carried only 200 passengers and lost $1 million, a very sizeable amount in those days. That same year, Raymond Whitcomb had also chartered the *Normandie* for a cruise to the Caribbean and Rio de Janeiro. It was a complete sell-out and earned $2 million. That money saved Raymond Whitcomb.

Both superliners were laid up at Bremerhaven as the Second World War exploded in the autumn of 1939. There were rumours that they would be converted to aircraft carriers or be fitted-out for use as landing ships for the projected Nazi sea invasion of England. In fact, the *Bremen* was swept by a fire, started by an unhappy cabin boy, on 16 March 1941. Her scorched remains were later broken up. The *Europa*, long idle and neglected, was seized by invading American forces at Bremerhaven in May 1945. Ultimately, she was allocated to the French to become the *Liberté*, sailing again on the North Atlantic (1950–61) until delivered to Italian scrappers in the winter of 1962.

Superliners remained a great part of steamship company thinking into the 1930s, despite the decisive Wall Street Crash of October 1929 and the

Another view of the library on board the 51,656grt *Bremen* (Hapag-Lloyd).

The mighty *Europa* returns to the Blohm & Voss Shipyard at Hamburg – and with a Hamburg South America Line *Monte*-class ship in the lower left (Richard Faber Collection).

Said to be a test run for future military operations, the *Bremen* passed through the Panama Canal in 1939. She was the largest vessel yet to have transited the Canal (Hapag-Lloyd).

onset of the catastrophic Depression. By the end of the twenties, Cunard was planning a new supership (the *Queen Mary*), White Star was planning one as well (the projected but never created Oceanic) and, across the Channel, the French were making plans of their own, for the spectacular *Normandie*. They also had their biggest liner yet for South American service underway (*L'Atlantique* of 1931). Italy had two big liners on its drawing boards as well, while Canadian Pacific planned for their largest liners yet, one for the Atlantic and the other for the Pacific. Shipyards remained quite busy, at least for the immediate future. Orders carried over. There were many other but more moderately sized passenger liners in the planning stages as well – including the largest yet for the likes of P&O, the US-flag Matson Line, and the largest for the Dutch colonial East Indies trade.

Passenger ships remained the great link – they were 'the only way to go'.

BIBLIOGRAPHY

Braynard, Frank O. & Miller, William H., *Picture History of the Cunard Line 1840–1990* (Courier Dover Publications, 1991).

Kludas, Arnold, *Great Passenger Ships of the World, Vol. II* (Stephens, 1976).

Kludas, Arnold, *Great Passenger Ships of the World, Vol. III* (Stephens, 1986).

Miller, William H., *Great British Passenger Ships* (The History Press, 2010).

Miller, William H., *Going Dutch: The Holland America Line Story* (Carmania Press, 1998).

Miller, William H., *Picture History of British Ocean Liners: 1900 to the Present* (Courier Dover Publications, 2001).

Miller, William H., *Picture History of the Cunard Line 1840–1990* (Courier Dover Publications, 1991).

Miller, William H., *Picture History of the French Line* (Courier Dover Publications, 1997).

Miller, William H., *Picture History of German and Dutch Passenger Ships* (Courier Dover Publications, 2002).

Miller, William H., *Picture History of the Italian Line* (Courier Dover Publications, 1999).

Miller, William H., *Pictorial Encyclopedia of Ocean Liners, 1860–1994* (Courier Dover Publications, 1995).

Miller, William H., *The First Great Ocean Liners in Photographs 1897–1927* (Courier Dover Publications, 1984).